LE DIFESE ATOMICHE DELLE POTENZE NUCLEARI NON IMPEDIRONO

IL RITORNO DI
GORGO

JOHN WEMBLEY · KENY SAHARA · DICK KENNEDY · CHARLES SIMON

IN ALTA DA ISHIRO HONDA

UNA COPRODUZIONE PATRIZIA CINEMATOGRAFICA · ACQUARIUS CINEMATOGRAFICA   COLORE DELLA TELECOLOR

THE LOST FILMS FANZINE PRESENTS MOVIE MILESTONES, VOL. 2, #4 SPRING 2021

EDITOR AND PUBLISHER: JOHN LEMAY/BICEP BOOKS SPECIAL CONSULTANT: KYLE BYRD

3

REPTILICUS

BURIED IN THE AGELESS FROZEN MUCK OF LAPLAND, THE SKELETAL REMNANTS OF AN UNKNOWN CREATURE WHICH ROAMED THE EARTH COUNTLESS EONS AGO LAY UN-DISTURBED AS HISTORY BEGAN AND MAN CAME INTO BEING! THERE WERE BONES DEEP BELOW THE TUNDRA. SOME FLESH, BUT NO LIFE AS SUCH! WHEN MINING EN-GINEER SVEND ALSTRUP SENT HIS DRILL DEEP BELOW THE SKIN OF THE EARTH, HE WAS SEEKING COPPER... BUT, WHAT HE FOUND WAS THAT WHICH BECAME REP-TILICUS! A MONSTER MORE THAN 100 FEET IN LENGTH, WITH LIMITLESS STRENGTH, AND SO ARMORED THAT NO WEAPON MAN COULD DEVISE WAS CAPABLE OF ENDING HIS AWESOME REIGN OF TERROR ON THE SCANDINAVIAN PENINSULA!

1961 will forever remain a unique year for fans of giant monster movies—specifically those of the "rubber suit" variety. And no, I'm not talking about monsters from Japan. That year saw no Godzilla movies released, but it did see the release of *Mothra*. (No, that doesn't count as rubber-suited either, as Mothra was brought to life via marionette.) 1961 is unique because it saw the release of three one-hit wonders from Europe, all brought to life via suitmation/marionettes despite being made in an era dominated by stopmotion monsters. I am talking, of course, about *Gorgo, Konga*, and *Reptilicus*.

Gorgo saw its release first, ironically enough premiering in Tokyo, Japan, on January 10, 1961. It would make its debut in the USA a few months later, on March 29th. It didn't see release in Great Britain, the country where it was predominantly set, until late October, oddly enough. *Reptilicus* was released on February 20, 1961, in Denmark but wouldn't make it to the U.S. until two years later in March of 1963. *Konga* premiered just a week before *Gorgo* in the U.S., on March 22nd. (As you can see all three films came out in the first part of 1961.)

Of the three, *Gorgo* is universally regarded as the best, and it's no wonder why. It had the highest production values and the most unique story in terms of a mother monster out to rescue her infant from a circus. Though inspired by King Kong, it was a great twist on the mythos. Also inspired by *King Kong* was *Konga*. However, *Konga* is really more along the lines of *I Was a Teenage Werewolf* in terms of its formula, and for most of the movie the monster is human-sized. In reality, the giant Konga doesn't do much city wrecking and only becomes gigantic for the very last bit of the movie. And then there's poor *Reptilicus*. The movie as written by Ib Melchior had a lot of potential that was bungled in the shooting process, by both the special effects and the acting. The pathetic puppet monster, on a par with *The Giant Claw*, is truly bizarre when juxtaposed in with the real military footage shot exclusively for the movie itself.

Of the three, *Gorgo* is my own unabashed favorite, as I saw it first, and at a young age to boot. I was also fortunate enough to see *Reptilicus* at an age young enough that I could sort of suspend disbelief as to that awful puppet, but just barely. Poor *Konga* though, I did not see until I was thirteen. So, while I love the idea of a *King Kong*-inspired film from the early Sixties, I can't say that I love the movie itself. In any case, despite the fact that *Gorgo* is arguably the only truly good movie of the bunch, all three are still very well-remembered to this day.

The three share similarities other than just being one-hit-wonders. Prior to their releases, all three received tie-in novelizations by Monarch Movie Books. (Notoriously, all three novelizations sexed up the storylines considerably!) Each monster also received a movie adaptation by Charlton Comics, which in turn led into ongoing series for each (though shortened in Reptilicus's case). So, even though the monsters never received on screen sequels, monster kids of the 1960s at least got to see them fight other monsters and assorted aliens in the comics.

On the note of the comics and novelizations, they will not be covered in-depth in this issue. My friend Allen Debus has written on all three extensively in publications like *G-Fan* and in his books like *Prehistoric Monster Mash* and *Dinosaurs in Fantastic Fiction*. Furthermore, *Bare Bones* #4 (another digest magazine with an issue largely devoted to *Gorgo, Konga*, and *Reptilicus*) has two bang-up excellent articles on the films in comic and novel form by Peter Enfantino which I suggest picking up as quickly as you can!

Back to this issue, this being a spin-off of *The Lost Films Fanzine*, this 'zine will also delve into the unmade aspects of these films, including deleted scenes and unmade sequels, of which, surprisingly, there aren't many. There were some interesting proto-versions of the films we will explore, though, like *Kuru Island, The Volcano Monsters*, and *I Was a Teenage Gorilla*.

So, if you're a fan of these movies like me--or if not the films themselves, then the idea of them at least---I hope you enjoy this tribute issue for the monsters of '61 on their 60th anniversary!

-John LeMay, March 2021

GORGO

Release Date: March 29, 1961 (U.S.)

DIRECTED BY: Eugène Lourié SPECIAL EFFECTS BY: Tom Howard SCREEN-PLAY BY: Robert L. Richards, Daniel James & Eugène Lourié (story) MUSIC BY: Angelo Francesco Lavagnino CAST: Bill Travers (Captain Joe Ryan) William Sylvester (Sam Slade) Vincent Winter (Sean) Christopher Rhodes (Harbour Master) Joseph O'Conor (Professor Hendricks) Bruce Seton (Professor Flaherty) Martin Benson (Dorkin)

Spherical, Technicolor, 78 Minutes

SYNOPSIS While searching for treasure off the coast of Ireland's Nara Island, Captain Joe Ryan and his ship barely survive a volcanic eruption at sea. Ryan and his friend/first officer, Sam Slade, come ashore to make arrangements for repairs. There they meet the harbor master and his young ward, Sean. Not long after, an enormous sea monster surfaces and attacks the village before being driven away. Ryan and Slade make a deal to capture the creature in return for a share of some of the hidden treasure found in the area. Slade and Ryan capture the monster via a huge net, and then transport it back to London, where it is slated to be sold to Dorkin's Circus. Unbeknownst to the men, Sean has stowed away to keep the monster company. As such, when they arrive in England, Sean becomes the two men's ward. The monster is given the moniker of Gorgo and becomes a popular attraction at the circus. It's eventually learned that little Gorgo is only an infant, and his mother, Ogra, is on her way to London. The even more massive Ogra surfaces and destroys most of London on her way to the circus. Meanwhile, Sean is lost in the chaos and rescued by Ryan, while Ogra rescues Gorgo. Despite the best efforts of the military, the mother monster and her infant make their way safely back to the sea and disappear.

OVERVIEW: Although it's not a Japanese giant monster movie, *Gorgo* has often been lumped in with the genre due to the fact that the title creation was a suitmation monster in an era known for stopmotion. In fact, *Gorgo* was a trilogy capper of sea monster movies that had begun with *The Beast from 20,000 Fathoms*, which was released in 1953 and inspired *Godzilla* in 1954. *Beast* was followed by *The Giant Behemoth*, released in 1959. Both of those monsters were stopmotion creations, but then came the suitmation *Gorgo* in 1961 from the same man who had directed the previous two pictures: Eugène Lourié. And though he did his best to avoid *Godzilla* comparisons, *Gorgo*'s climax seems like a color remake of *Godzilla* at times.

Actually, *Gorgo* is inspired by Godzilla movies more than most people realize. In 1957, movie producers the King

Brothers distributed Toho's *Rodan* in the U.S. to great success. As such, they wanted to make their own Japanese monster movie with the unique idea that a monster be captured by the circus (which actually isn't that unique, it's more of a callback to *King Kong*). The King Bros teamed with a mystery Japanese studio (probably Toho, though it's never been confirmed) and recruited the services of Lourié to write and direct. Lourié conceived of a story that served as a precedent to movies like *Mothra* (1961) and *Gappa, the Triphibian Monster* (1967), in that the monster was a protagonist of sorts rather than an antagonist. The reason was that Lourié's daughter chastised him for killing the title creature in *Beast*, and so he vowed to rectify that complaint by making a movie where the monster lived. To that end he cooked up *Kuru Island*, a simple tale where a baby monster is captured on a south seas island and brought to a Tokyo Zoo. The mama monster would come to the rescue, and

notably, there would be no big military confrontations. The King Bros liked everything but the lack of military spectacle, and so they added that element in to Lourié's disdain. The Japanese producers had also backed out, and so the Japanese locale was discarded. However, the King Bros were still keen on using the Japanese method of a man in a suit to bring their monster to life.

While Lourié attended to other matters, such as making sure that the suit was superior to the one in *Godzilla*, a new writer punched up the script, eliminating the Japanese characters and setting. The story was relocated to Ireland and England (though Australia and Paris were considered at one point). Lourié's original characters, a group of pearl divers, were retrofitted to become weary sailors who capture a monster. To that end, Lourié's original theme about reverence for nature became about man's insatiable greed. And, as the King Bros wanted, scenes of the mother monster fighting the military were added.

Though Lourié may have been disappointed in the new screenplay and military scenes, he succeeded in making a suitmation monster that beat its Japanese inspirations. As it stands, the Gorgo suit is leagues better than Toho's Godzilla suit. Heresy for some, sure, but true nonetheless. And while I will go so far as to say that Gorgo's suit was executed better than Godzilla's on a technical front, I will at least say that it's debatable who had the better design. In terms of depiction, Godzilla was a tough act to follow, nor could Gorgo too closely resemble Toho's creation. Adding to the design challenge would be the fact that, like Godzilla, Gorgo would have to be an upright man-in-suit dinosaur (quadrupeds were tough to do in suits). As such, Lourié made sure the creature had no dorsal plates or fins along its back. (Instead, the two monsters have armored backs, similar to a later Toho creation named Baragon.) To set him/her apart from both Godzilla and a run of the mill theropod dinosaur, Gorgo was given a very distinct trait in the form of the two fin-like ears atop the head. Gorgo and Ogra also have extremely large hands when compared to Godzilla and Toho's other monsters. (This was probably to show how Gorgo could swim through the water with ease.) As stated before, Ogra's attack on London looks like an updated, color version of Godzilla in certain scenes as the monster demolishes various landmarks and plows through electrical lines. The lighting of these sequences, particularly the colorful smoke in the background, are breathtaking for any special effects fan.

On that note, Gorgo mostly succeeds on a technical level. That is to say, most people remember the film for the effects more so than the script. As it stands, the story in some ways is just a twist on King Kong: a monster is captured in a distant land and chaos ensues when it comes to the mainland. The twist in Gorgo's case is that the monster is a baby rather than a full-grown adult, and that it survives the movie's end. Other than that novelty to set it apart, Gorgo's story is a bit odd in that there are no female characters (other than Ogra, but she doesn't really talk). Not that there's anything wrong with a film's characters comprising of only women or only men, but it should suit the story when it does. In Gorgo's case, the film seems to be lacking a woman's touch. Not that we needed another forced, out of place romance, but there was probably an opportunity to have a character who is a mother to act as a voice of sorts for Ogra, who only wants her baby back. There was a good opportunity for that too, with the orphan Sean playing a large part in the film. Other than that small quibble, Gorgo is still one of the best monster movies of the 1960s.

The film was an expensive endeavor for the King Bros, who went so far as to create full-scale Gorgo props (again-- Gorgo--not massive mama Ogra). These gigantic props, perhaps more than anything, are what helped the film to outshine its Japanese inspirations. (In paticular, the Gorgo hand prop rising out of the water to overturn a boat in a spooky, nighttime scene is spectacular) When all was said and done, the King Bros had spent $650,000 (the budget of 1933's King Kong, coincidentally) to shoot the movie. They spent even more to market the film, which upped their final tally to over $2 million. As it turned out, Gorgo's production was so massive (and troublesome) that it actually led to the delay/cancellation of 30 other King Brothers films! And, even though the film finished shooting in December of 1959, its release was delayed by nearly two years. Ironically enough, it premiered in Tokyo on January 10, 1961, where it became a massive hit in Japan. It was unleashed in the U.S. a few months later, and in the U.K. in the Fall.

"Very often, a charmingly naive Frank King asks me if I could see a method to make a life-size gigantic Gorgo walking on London streets. I humor him. 'But think, Frank, about engineering problems to build a moving beast the size of the Eiffel Tower!' The next day, pursuing his dreams, he comes in with a new idea; 'What if we make it in rubber filled with air, like the Macy's Parade?' Ideas filled with hot air—producer's prerogatives." Eugène Lourié, FANTASTIC FILMS

DAS HAT DIE WELT NOCH NICHT GESEHEN!

METRO-GOLDWYN-MAYER
and
KING BROTHERS present

GORGO

BILL TRAVERS · WILLIAM SYLVESTER

by EUGENE LOURIE · FRANK KING and MAURICE KING

TECHNICOLOR

Finally the beast is captured, to the chagrin of young Vincent Winter.

Metro-Goldwyn-Mayer presents
A King Brothers production "GORGO" in Technicolor

In an era of stop motion monsters, 1961's *Gorgo* always stood out in the west because the monster was brought to life through the distinctly Japanese suitmation technique. Perhaps it shouldn't come as a surprise then that *Gorgo* actually has some roots in Japan. It all started with the King Brothers' very successful U.S. distribution of *Rodan*. As a result, they wanted to create their own giant monster. They also had a unique angle to their idea, that being that the giant monster be captured by a circus. The King Brothers made a deal with an unnamed Japanese studio, which was most likely Toho since they had worked with them to distribute *Rodan*. From what we can piece together, they secured a deal with the mystery studio in Japan sometime in 1958 (which makes sense, since *Rodan* was released in the U.S. in 1957 and had generated huge profits). With the U.S.-Japan co-production secured, the King Brothers next needed a director.

Due to his success directing *The Beast from 20,000 Fathoms* (1953) and *The Giant Behemoth* (1959), the King Brothers approached director Eugene Lourié. Lourié wasn't exactly itching to make another such film, and was actually working on another project that would ultimately go unmade. He told Paul

Mandell in *Fantastic Films* that, "This type of picture was not in my mind at the time—I had hoped to realize an ultra-modern science fiction story called *Moonwreck* which I had adapted from a British SF novel. But after some reflection, I saw many possible variations on the same theme—a helpless sea monster against a city. I also remembered, quite vividly, the incident with my daughter and *The Beast From 20,000 Fathoms*. Here was the occasion to repair my wrongs against the sea monster species!"

The incident that Lourie speaks of with his daughter involved a promise he had made to her after her disappointment in *The Beast's* ending. She had apparently told her father, "You are bad, Daddy. You killed the big nice Beast!" Lourié told Mandell that "I knew that someday I would have to write a story in which the creature does not die—it just goes away!"

The story, which was mandated to be set in Japan, was co-written with Lourié's friend and collaborator Daniel James (under the name David Hyatt) and was titled *Kuru Island*. It is similar to *Gorgo* but with a huge difference in location: it is set in Japan and the South Pacific. Interviewer Mandell described the story as being set on "a fictitious atoll in the South Pacific where cultured pearls were the main export. After a tremendous storm and an underwater

Page Opposite: Thai poster for GORGO. Above: Concept art depecting Ogra in a quadruped stance by Edgar Kiechle.

eruption, the baby creature surfaces and adheres [sic] to the island. Tidal waves and other phenomena mark the unbalancing of the environment. The beast was to have been captured and brought to a Tokyo zoo for observation when the mother beast surfaces to rescue it." The only other details known about the script was that it had a reverence for nature, a few of the main characters would be pearl divers, and the opening volcanic eruption seen in *Gorgo* was also present in *Kuru Island*. Bill Cooke's *Gorgo* book also offers a similar synopsis: "...an oceanic earthquake unleashes a sea monster that is captured by a couple of pearl divers off said island and brought to the Tokyo Zoo for study. But in a surprising plot development, the creature's much-larger parent soon surfaces, trampling through the city in search for her stolen offspring."

Setting the story in Japan was a mandate from the King Brothers, whose production partner at the time was a mystery Japanese studio that, to this day, has yet to be named. Lourié was keen on making a "poetic" non-violent monster film. He told Mandell, "I wanted the creature to confront human beings but there were no scenes of the military shooting at it and not being able to destroy it. That concept is really ridiculous... The creature was not supposed to destroy the town, and there were no stock shots planned of military intervention." The basis for Lourié's story was centered instead on motherly love over conflict with the military. He was sure the idea would appeal to the King Brothers, whom Lourié said, "I believe they had a bit of a mother complex." However, later when it would come time to shoot, the King Brothers made sure to add in plenty of city destruction and military battles.

Other than the previous statements, we unfortunately don't know much about more specific details of *Kuru Island*. It is said that the first treatment

LONDON TOWER.

Page Opposite: Lourié's concept drawing of Gorgo. Take note of the fact that the man holding the spear appears to be a pearl diver, and certainly doesn't look like a Nara Islander from Ireland. Above is a beautiful concept painting by Edgar Kiechle, by the time the story had shifted to London. Right: A closer detail on the head by Lourié.

was ten pages long, and that it was approved by the financers in Japan. In August of 1958, they began work on a full *Kuru Island* script and were allotted two months to complete it. In November of 1958, just as the duo were finishing up the last pages of the script, the deal fell through with the mystery Japanese studio and the King Brothers were on their own.

But who was the mystery Japanese studio? Like this magazine, the Japanese published *Tokusatsu Hihou* also firmly believes that the studio involved in *Kuru Island* was none other than Toho. As it was, Toho was the only Japanese studio at that time known for giant monster movies. Further proof that Toho was the mystery studio would

seem to be in a Godzilla manga in which Godzilla's child (not Minilla, he had yet to be created) is stranded in Tokyo and is rescued by his father. The only problem with this manga is that it predates *Kuru Island's* pre-production and was published in 1957.

The manga story is called "The Last Godzilla" and was written by Yoshiharu Hashimoto. It begins with an audience settling down in a theater to watch *Monster King Godzilla*. As the movie progresses and Godzilla shows up on-screen, the head of the real Godzilla bursts through the movie screen. The monster, in fact a juvenile Godzilla, crawls into the theater and chases out the patrons and then bursts out of the

Cover and interior panels for "The Last Godzilla" (1957). Take note how Godzilla and his son stomp through a Tokyo Zoo (in KURU ISLAND the monster was supposed to be taken to a Tokyo Zoo). Also note how the parent and child monsters wade out to sea together in one of the last panels to the left and right. Godzilla © Toho Co., LTd.

theater into the streets of the city. The nimble young kaiju climbs atop a building and the police begin to fire their guns at it. When it starts to breathe fire, the fire department shows up and pelts it with water. Off the coast, the adult Godzilla surfaces to retrieve his young and battles the military on his way into the city. Godzilla embraces his son atop the building and it climbs onto its father's back. Godzilla carries his child out of the city. The two Godzillas are next seen attacking a circus where animals run in fear and some are eaten. Many of the animals run loose through Tokyo as the U.S. military flies in from the skies. They launch a nuclear warhead at Godzilla in the heart of the city, but the monster catches it in midair. Godzilla then bites off part of the missile and throws the rest into the water.

The human aspect of the storyline is somewhat harder to follow, but it cen-

the deer and gets in a scuffle with the bad guy's henchmen. Emi frees the deer just as Godzilla and his child arrive, but the monsters cause no harm and head out to sea into the sunrise. (The manga was published in Shonen Magazine's *Omoshiro Book* for the October 1957 issue.)

As to why *Kuru Island* got dropped, it's interesting to note that Lourié stated that the Japanese end of the production fell through in November of 1958. Toho would have just released their newest kaiju film, *Varan*, into theaters. The film was not a hit at all. It had also began life as a U.S.-Japanese co-production where the U.S. backers deserted Toho. Perhaps the negative experience coupled with the box office failure of *Varan* is what caused Toho to back out of the project? Again, that's if it was Toho, but chances are extremely high that they were the studio.

And for one final question: If Toho had produced *Kuru Island* with the King Bros, does that mean we would have eventually seen *Godzilla vs. Gorgo*, or perhaps Gorgo in *Destroy All Monsters* (1967) ???

ters on a young couple, Masao and Emi, who are on a date in the theater when Godzilla shows up. Masao seems to have some sort of involvement with the government or gives them unsolicited advice. In one of the comic's more interesting scenes, a man arrives at the conference claiming to have yet another of the deceased Dr. Serizawa's heretofore unknown doomsday weapons—a type of poison gas. There is also a cigar-smoking villain of sorts who possibly has ideas of killing the Godzillas so that he can put their corpses on display. He tries to lure the monster to the beach with a deer (filled with poison) as bait. Masao tries to free

As it turned out, *Kuru Island* wasn't the King Brothers only axed monster movie with Toho. In the latter 1960s, Toho and the King Bros almost teamed to produce another sci-fi/monster picture as reported in *Castle of Frankenstein #10* in 1967. The report stated that the King Bros were working on a movie with Toho called "From the Depths" that was also based upon a nov-el. However, the clos-est novel I could find with that title was *Stranger From the Depths* (published in '67) about a Gillman of sorts.

I was about ready to give up until I stumbled across mention of a simi-lar King Bros proj-ect in an interview with stopmotion animator Jim Dan-forth. Danforth reported that in the early 1970s he was approached by the King Bros about adapting the novel *War with the Newts* by Karel Čapek. Furthermore, Danforth said that the King Bros had been trying to film it "for years" (by the early 1970s, 1967 would qualify as a "for years" I'd say). I looked into what *War with the Newts* was and found that it was more or less about a war with an underwater race of large, salaman-der-like creatures. This would seem far more fitting for Toho than the novel *Stranger from the Depths*. I have now come to believe that the aborted 1967 *From the Depths* was the new title that the King Bros gave to their hoped for adaptation of *War with the Newts*.

Though obscure today, back in the mid-1960s, the novel was well remem-bered. A satirical science fiction tale,

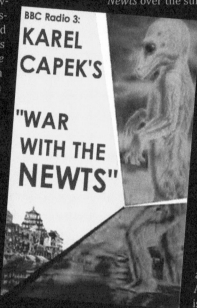

BBC Radio 3:
KAREL CAPEK'S

"WAR WITH THE NEWTS"

it was published in 1936 by the afore mentioned Czech writer Karel Čapek. At the time, Čapek's country was pre occupied with the developing state o National Socialism in Germany. As such his works at the time picked up on th fears and anxieties of the Czech peopl at the time. It is believed that this fea fed into the writing of *War with th Newts* over the summer of 1935. Čape based his story on the idea o the emergence o a new intelligen race, the Newts.

Divided into three sections, o books, Book One begins with th discovery of th titular Newts. The are found by a na val captain, Cap tain van Toch, or a small island nea Sumatra. These large intelligent Salaman-der-like beings are adept at pearl diving As such, their valu is immediately recog nized. Introduced to human civilization, they begin to devel op the ability to speak and slowly make their way into human society. Book One ends with the creation of The Salaman der Syndicate, overseen by a wealthy industrialist, Mr. Bondy, who intends to diversify the Newts into new areas o hydroengineering.

Though the first part of the story was light in tone overall, Book Two takes the Newts down a darker path. Entitled "U the Ladder of Civilization", we watch as the first hostilities between Newts and human beings develop. The book is told mostly via newspaper clippings, and things don't truly get interesting unti Book Three: War with the Newts. It be gins with a series of minor skirmishes

WAR WITH THE NEWTS

between the humans and the salamanders until it escalates into all-out war. The Newts plan to decimate entire sections of major continents as a way of creating new coastlines to increase their territory. Eventually one-fifth of the Earth's landmass is destroyed with humanity offering little resistance. By now, it looks as though when the war is over, most of Earth's landmasses will be all but destroyed, with the remaining humans left as slaves to work in the Newts' factories. The author ends his book predicting that eventually the Newts will form separate countries as mankind did and ultimately destroy themselves.

Towards the end of the writing process, Čapek summed up his last chapter on August 27, 1935, stating, "Today I completed the last chapter of my utopian novel. The protagonist of this chapter is nationalism. The content is quite simple: the destruction of the world and its people. It is a disgusting chapter, based solely on logic. Yet it had to end this way. What destroys us will not be a cosmic catastrophe but mere reasons of state, economics, prestige, etc." Due to the fact that the book poked fun of and exposed the evils of the Nazi party, it was naturally banned in 1940s Germany.

The King Bros were obviously fond of the tale, hence their trying to get it off the ground for many years. To date, it remains un-adapted in the film medium.

Toho of Japan has co-productions with the United States lined up. With the King Brothers (who made **GORGO** and **CAPTAIN SINDBAD** Toho will film **FROM THE DEPTHS**, a script from the sci-fi novel of the same title. With Allied Artists will be a film tentatively titled **THE KILLING BOTTLE**, starring Nick Adams and Akira Takarada. (Last summer in Japan, Adams made **FRANKENSTEIN CONQUERS THE WORLD** for Toho/AIP.) The third film, for Henry G. Saperstein Enterprises, is titled **THE FRANKENSTEIN BROTHERS** (what is poor Frank coming to?) with Tab **WAR-GODS OF THE DEEP**) Hunter . . .

Page Opposite: Ad for BBC production of the novel. This page, above right: Cover for the novel. Above: Blurb from CASTLE OF FRANKENSTEIN #10 C.1967.

LOCATION, LOCATION, LOCATION!

Beautiful concept art of Ogra attacking Paris as drawn by Edgar Kiechle. Before Paris, the King Bros also considered having the monster attack Australia. However, they decided against it because "there are no monuments in Australia, and besides, who cares if a monster destroys Australia?" According to Lourié, Rome and Madrid were also considered for a time.

Once the Japanese studio was out, the King Brothers no longer had any interest in setting or shooting the picture in Japan. Lourié remembered to Paul mandell that, "After living intensely with my Japanese and Pacific native characters for two months, it was impossible for me to do a rewrite and change the locale to some European country." Or, in other words, *Kuru Island* was culturally tailored to Japan, and retrofitting the story wouldn't be as simple as switching the locales to another country. (I don't know of any pearl divers off the coast of Ireland, do you?)

Rather than Lourié, it was the King Brothers who started brainstorming ideas for alternate locations. Specifically, they had their sights set on Paris. In an interview with Art Buchwald in his column on May 18, 1959, Maurice King told him, "We're going to destroy Paris like it's never been destroyed before. Frank's dying to because of the prices. But Paris has something. Tokyo's already been destroyed [on-screen and in real life], and so has Berlin. And King Kong wrecked New York." King also added that, "In trying to find her baby, [the mother monster] wrecks the Eiffel Tower, the Arc de Triomphe, the Louvre, the Opera, the Grand Palais and two bridges on the Seine."

However, only Lourié thought through the realities of the scenario. Louire said, "During my meetings with the King brothers, they expressed their desire to have the climax happen in Paris. 'Think, Gene,' pleaded Frank King, 'how spectacular it would be if the monster were to climb the Eiffel Tower!' When I told him that Paris is at least 250 miles from the sea, he doubted my words."

In searching for a new location, London was the one finally slated for demolition. Elsewhere, a new writer, Robert L. Richards under the alias of John Loring, was hired to verhaul *Kuru Island* to match the new characters and settings. Many of the ideas were retained, such as opening with a volcanic eruption, the mother and baby monster, and so on. What differed was the removal of Lourié's theme of inbalance of nature. The new theme inserted by Loring was the peril of humanity's greed. The new writer also inserted exactly what the King Brothers had wanted from the beginning: military on monster action, which Lourié had been reluctant to include. Upon reading the new script, Lourié almost wanted to reject it. "It was enough to make me lose heart over the project. But I wanted to direct the film," Lourié told Mandell.

Though it's unknown what the monster's name had been in *Kuru Island*, now it was Gorgo, so named after the Gorgosaurus ("a gigantic carnivore saurian that lived during the Upper Cretaceous and resembled the Tyrannosaurus Rex", according to a Dr. J. Augusta in a book on prehistoric animals).

Lourié said of the finished *Gorgo* script, "The story as originally conceived was far more poetic. But the King Brothers butchered the idea entirely." Lourié also cut the film together to his liking, and then had to go on to work another job in early 1960. During this time, the King Brothers recut the film the way they wanted, adding in a multitude of military stock shots. "[Depth] charges were being dropped, planes criss-crossed the skies, explosives were added! When I expressed my doubts to the King brothers, they assured me that they knew the taste of audiences better than me... maybe they knew?"

Lourié was so disappointed with the additions of graphic city destruction and military conflict that in later years, he even edited his own version of *Gorgo*! He told Mandell, "I recently acquired an old print of *Gorgo*...and made a 35-minute version by taking out all those unnecessary scenes. Everything was so much better." This cut was created during the year 1980 (or possibly sometime prior), but no one knows if it was ever shown in any official capacity.

Gorgo had several ambitious scripted scenes that were never filmed such as a scuffle with a giant octopus that may have been present in the *Kuru Island* script. The scene was to have Joe and Sam diving amongst a graveyard of Viking ships only to be pursued by a killer whale. As the duo hides out in one of the ships, they find it to be home to a giant octopus, which naturally attacks them. After struggling in the grasp of the beast's tentacles, baby Gorgo makes his entrance shrouded by a cloud of ink from the octopus:

BACK TO SCENE - ANOTHER ANGLE - THE TWO   59
as Joe charges in, CAMERA MOVING with him. Sam has dropped his flare, and it now lies a little distance below on the rocky bottom. As Joe comes in, another tentacle whips out for him, and now we can see the huge, dirty-green body of the thing and its great, staring, saucer-eyes. But Joe does not make the mistake of trying to avoid the tentacle. He fights only to keep his arms and gun free, and rides in with the snake-like arm, Intent only on getting in close enough for a killing shot. Sam by now is almost help¬less. With a half-Imprisoned arm, he is trying to cut through a truck tire with a Jackknife. Another tentacle has coiled around Joe, but he drives in.

And now, straight between the eyes of the thing, he fires. There is a dull, muffled explosion (the ex¬ploding tip of the harpoon). The great octopus shudders violently, its color changes rapidly from the dirty-green to a reddish-brown, its tentacles loosen and become limp, and, as the two men struggle free, in its death agony, it emits a great, jetting cloud of black ink, all but obliterating the scene. Joe and Sam pull back a little, close together.

CLOSE SHOT – JOE 60
his anxious face seen through his face plate, looking at Sam.

TWO SHOT   61
as Sam, exhausted, nevertheless gestures that he's okay. Now the two look around, looking upward through the murk, the killer whale not forgotten.
WHAT THEY SEE: 62
dimly through the darkly clouded waters, a shadow passing over. The whale has not forgotten them.

BACK TO SCENE   63
as Joe gestures caution. They are in no shape for another fight at the moment. From his belt, Joe gets another charge for the harpoon gun, loads it. Prom somewhat below, the flare glows dimly. Then suddenly there is a tremendous, thrashing turmoil in the water above them. They look up quickly, SEE:

WHAT THEY SEE: 64
Through the murk and the wildly turbulent water, they can see only something fantastically big and vague, like a great thundercloud. The water is whipped to fury. Then all at once there is a great jetting gush of blood that crimsons the water all around, blotting out everything in a swirling red haze.

BACK TO SCENE   65
as the two cling to the rook formation, staring up-wards, staring at each other.

Fantastic Films alludes to the scene being filmed as Mandell wrote that "For an early sequence in *Gorgo* where divers are attacked by an octopus, a deep tank was used on the main stage." Though we can't find any evidence of the scene being shot, it was at least included in the film's comic book adaptation, the panels of which are reproduced in the following pages.

SAM, YOU'RE THINKIN' 'BOUT THE DEAD MEN! IF YOU DON'T WANTA DIVE, DON'T!

I'M GOIN' DOWN ALL RIGHT! TO SEE THAT *YOU* COME BACK UP ALL RIGHT!

GOLD... VIKING GOLD WAS THE LURE THAT TOOK THE ADVENTURERES DOWN INTO THE ACCURED GAELIC COVE...

JOE DIDN'T TRY TO EVADE THE OCTOPUS OR THE CRUSHING TENTACLE LOOPING AROUND HIM ! HE WENT CLOSER, AIMING THE EXPLOSIVE HARPOON CAREFULLY FOR THE ONE CHANCE THEY'D HAVE ...

BOOM!

THE KILLER WHALE HAD DECIDED... THEY WERE NEXT ON HIS INCREDIBLE MENU! THIS TIME, THE TWO KNEW THE PERIL WAS GREAT INDEED ...

ER... AS WATER IS BEING PUMPED ABOARD THE TRITON, SAM SLADE AND JOE RYAN WATCH E ISLANDERS' ACTIVITIES IN THE GROWING DUSK...

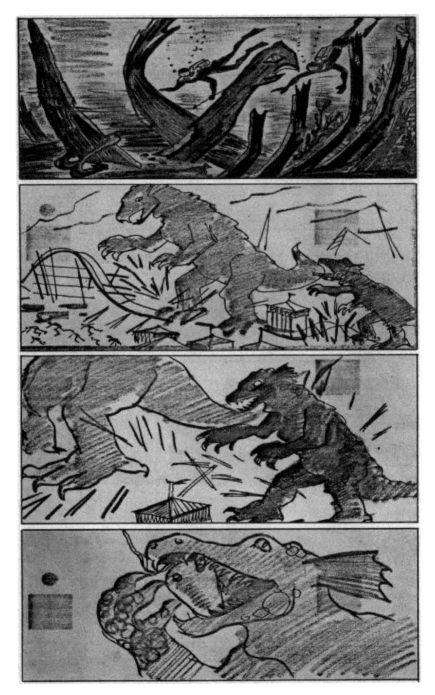

Other unfilmed scenes included baby Gorgo scuffling with a circus elephant and Ogra destroying a lighthouse.

In 1967, Nikkatsu released GAPPA, THE TRIPHIBIAN MONSTER, which featured a baby monster being taken from a Pacific island to Japan. The two parent monsters then come to the mainland to rescue it. Since it is so similar to GORGO, some have wondered if the mystery Japanese studio behind KURU ISLAND was Nikkatsu. However, back in 1958, Nikkatsu wasn't known for special effects films—nor were they in 1967, which is why they brought in Toho's Akira Watanabe to handle the special effects. Furthermore, GAPPA writers Gan Yamazaki and Ryuzo Nakanishi were quoted in the book MONSTERS ARE ATTACKING TOKYO as saying that they had never even seen GORGO!

The same year that GAPPA was unleashed, Toho gave the Big G an heir in SON OF GODZILLA, which other than featuring a parent and child monster relationship, wasn't similar to GORGO. Years later, in 1977, SON OF GODZILLA was released in Italy as THE RETURN OF GORGO! In addition to this, Gorgo/Ogra has himself/herself been retrofitted in posters to resemble Japanese monsters. In the top poster, she's been given dorsal plates like Godzilla, while the bottom poster appears to show the flying turtle Gamera as Ogra!!!

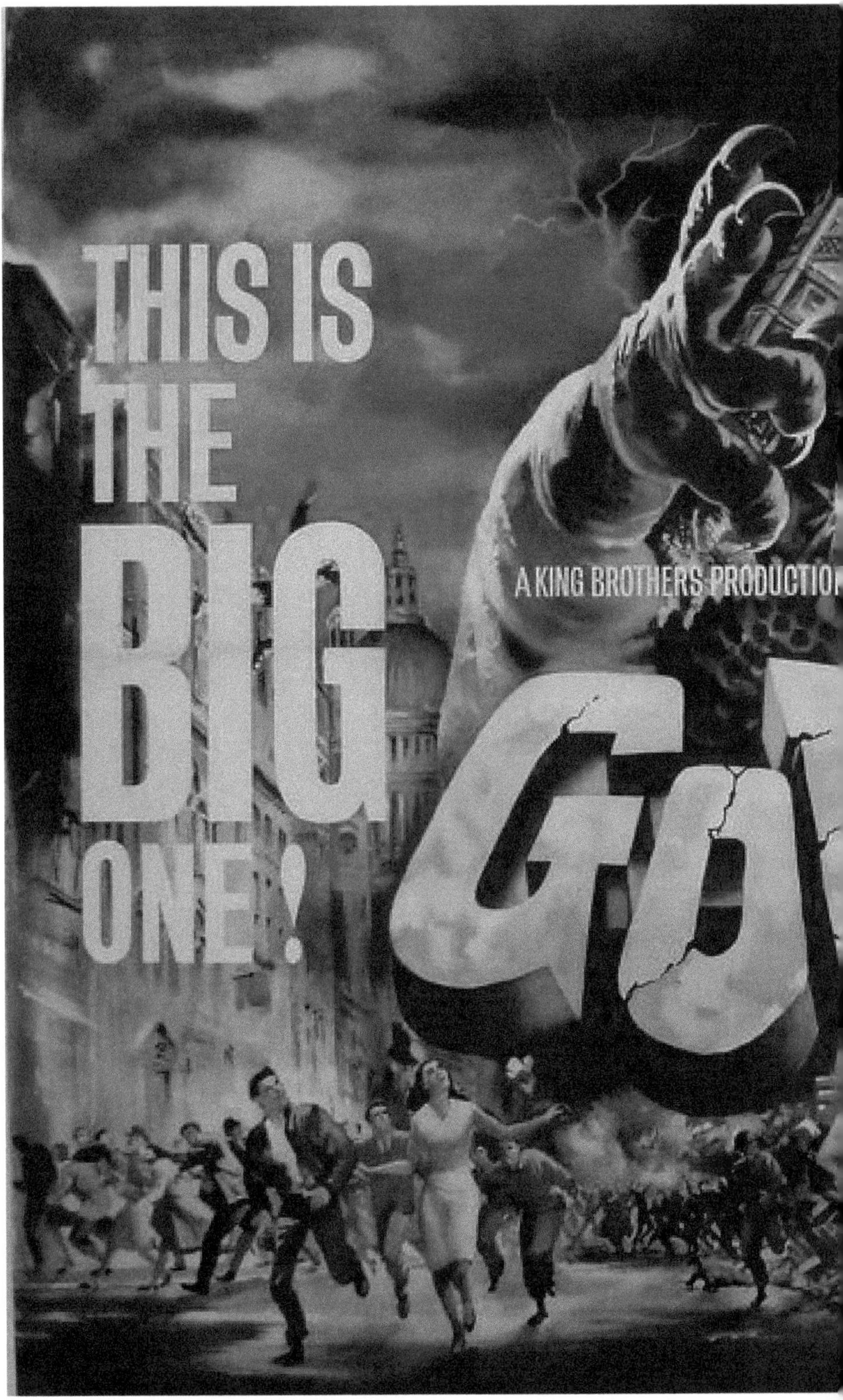
THIS IS
THE
BIG
ONE!
A KING BROTHERS PRODUCTION

starring
BILL TRAVERS
WILLIAM SYLVESTER

TECHNICOLOR

X

REPTILICUS

Release Date:
February 20, 1961 (Denmark)
January 1963 (U.S.)

DIRECTED BY: Sid Pink [U.S. version]
Poul Bang [Danish version] SPECIAL
EFFECTS BY: Kai Koed & Orla Høyer
SCREENPLAY BY: Ib Melchior & Sid
Pink MUSIC BY: Sven Gyldmark CAST:
Carl Ottosen (General Mark Grayson)
Ann Smyrner (Lise Martens) Mimi
Heinrich (Karen Martens) Bent Mej-
ding (Svend Viltorft) Asbjørn Andersen
(Professor Otto Martens) Bodil Miller
(Connie Miller) [Danish version] Marla
Behrens (Connie Miller) [American
version] Povl Wøldike (Dr. Peter Dalby)
Dirch Passer (Peterson) Ole Wisborg
(Captain Brandt)

Spherical, Pathécolor, 82 Minutes
(U.S.) 92 Minutes (Denmark)

SYNOPSIS: As a mining crew drills into the earth, they bore into the still fresh remains of a prehistoric monster. A severed tail is found and transported to Copenhagen, where it is studied by Professor Otto Martens. There too is the man who discovered it, Svend Viltorft, who falls in love with Marten's young-est daughter Karen. When the sample begins to regenerate into a new life-form, General Mark Grayson is called in to keep an eye on it. Eventually the specimen, dubbed Reptilicus, grows too large to be contained and escapes. It ravages the countryside and develops strange new abilities (flight in the Dan-ish version and green acid in the U.S. cut). Professor Martens becomes de-spondent when explosives are used on the monster and has a heartattack. Mar-tens is smart enough to realize that if the monster is blown to bits more mon-sters will spawn from its remains. As such, it is decided to launch a massive tranquilizer into the monster's mouth as it attacks Copenhagen. Grayson fires the shot, knocking the monster out so that it can be destroyed thoroughly. However, on the ocean floor, a severed foot belonging to the monster is already spawning.

OVERVIEW: *Reptilicus* is a classic ex-ample of a terrible monster movie that monster kids desperately want to like. Well, actually, quite a few do like it... but what I'm trying to say is that even though *Reptilicus* has an awesome con-cept, a drop-dead gorgeous movie post-er, and a well-designed monster—all those things are positively obliterated by the terrible Reptilicus puppet itself. I suppose it's a bit like *The Giant Claw.* Not really that bad of a movie so much as a bad prop that completely lets it down. As it stands, both the creators of the film and the audience alike deserved a better executed monster. But, at the same time, the bad monster might just be part of *Reptilicus's* charm.

Reptilicus began life with *The Angry Red Planet* (1959), a hit release for American International Pictures, which was written and directed by Ib Melchior and produced by Sid Pink. AIP wanted more pictures from the duo and signed them up for two more. And, because Melchior and Pink both had connections to Denmark, it was decided to shoot the two new pictures there in conjunction with AIP and Danish studio, Saga Productions.

One of the films would be similar to *The Angry Red Planet*, and was titled *Journey to the Seventh Planet*, and the other was an as yet unnamed monster movie. Like the King Bros with *Gorgo*, AIP was encouraged by the giant monster genre from Japan in suggesting a giant monster flick (they may have been aware of *Gorgo's* production, too).

When AIP suggested this, Melchior essentially created a new storyline out of two lost projects. For the basic story structure and characters, he resuscitated an old script called *The Volcano Monsters* (see the section devoted to this starting on page 42). The other

was a non-monster movie Melchior had dreamed up that had to do with scientists creating a serum that could regenerate severed limbs and body parts (the idea being to create an "indestructible society"). That idea had come to him from the regenerative properties of starfish and lizards, the latter of which has the ability to regenerate its severed tail. In this case, Melchior decided to do the opposite, the severed tail would regenerate into a new monster!

His opening scene, where the tail is discovered by a mining crew, was also lifted from another unproduced script from 1958 called *The Micro-Men*. (The unmade story told of an ancient meteor, buried underground, that is found to contain microscopic spores of intelligence that virally infect the discoverers to take over their minds). According to Melchior, AIP's rather unimaginative story pitch simply had the monster showing up from out of nowhere, and Melchior felt the regeneration idea would set the story apart, and it did.

The initial story meeting had occurred in early March, and by March 14th, AIP

INVINCIBLE...
INDESTRUCTIBLE!
What was this BEAST
born fifty million
years out of time?

IN COLOR

CARL OTTOSEN
ANN SMYRNER
SID PINK · IB MELCHIOR · SID PINK
SIDNEY PINK

A CINEMAGIC, INC. PRODUCTION

Top: Lise Martens, played by Ann Smyrner above, was originally supposed to be played by Nora Hayden. Inset: Dirch Passer, left, was so popular at the time that Saga Studios flirted with titling their version of the film DIRCH AND THE DRAGON!

had officially greenlit the story. Melchior, being fluid in Danish and English, was supposed to get to direct the English version of the film. But, for some strange reason, Pink directed it instead. (In retrospect, perhaps Melchior should be glad that he did!) The reason for the switch may have been due to the Danish production partner, Saga Studios, which Pink had connections to.

Reptilicus is also unique because two distinct versions of the film were planned from the beginning. (Unlike *Godzilla, King of the Monsters!,* where new actors were inserted later.) Two versions of the film would be shot simultaneously with Pink directing the English language version, and Poul Bang directing the Danish version (though Pink reportedly hovered in the background to backseat direct!). Basically, the same actors filmed their scenes twice. Once for the Danish version and

again for the English speaking version. As such, you can watch the same scenes not just in a different language, but from different angles and with different dialogue. (See later in the issue for a more detailed comparison.)

The film was shot in the summer of 1960 over 86 days. Denmark welcomed the production with open arms, allowing the producers the needed publicity to generate extras for the "panicked crowd" shots necessary for any giant monster flick. (Around a thousand extras participated in the famous drawbridge scene, including the Bicycle Club which happily agreed to plummet into the waters below – so apparently those weren't trained stuntmen!) Also thanks to Saga Studios owner, Fleming John Olsen, who had a great deal of influence in the Social Democratic Party, the Danish Army and Navy were used extensively for the battle scenes. In other words, all the military footage is new, unlike *Gor-*

Kaj Koed shows off Reptilicus miniature amid scale model of Copenhagen, soon to be destroyed.

THE LOST PROP? According to Danish publicity materials from the time, a 32-foot-long Reptilicus model was created which had the ability to shoot smoke from its nostrils and had flashing eyes. It would seem this was either an invention of the press or something that went unused entirely though the former is more likely. Most likely, the two props seen above were all that existed.

go's stock shots. As such, *Reptilicus* has a grand polished look unbefitting of its Z-Grade monster puppet.

As it was, the Danish effects technicians from Saga were not up to the task of creating a convincing monster. Reptilicus certainly had a cool design, it just wasn't brought to life adequately. (It wouldn't even pass muster in a peplum movie where it wasn't the focus of the story!) Going off of rare behind the scenes photos, the two Reptilicus puppets looked to be between four to seven feet long. (Truthfully, had they really cared about the film, they should have scrapped the existing footage and hired Ray Harryhausen to create the monster in post-production.)

When the film premiered in Denmark in February of 1961, it was not surprisingly met with laughter and heckling. Reviews were naturally also poor. When AIP executive/founder Samuel

Z. Arkoff saw the film he was mortified, not only by the monster but by the performances as well. Since the actors were Danish, they therefore had thick Danish accents in all of their scenes. As such, the English footage would still have to be dubbed over to mask the thick accents of most of the cast. (In a way, they shot it twice for nothing, the only benefit in this method was that the mouths would at least match the words coming out of them unlike the Godzilla movies.) For a time, AIP decided not to distribute the movie at all, hence the fact that Pink sued them. However, when Pink's own lawyer looked at the awful footage he advised Pink to drop the case!

However, Arkoff eventually talked to Melchior about the troubled film, asking him if he thought it was possible to save it through a recut. Melchior told Brett Homenick on Vantage Point Interviews:

THE LOST CUT Today, the original English language audio has never surfaced, making it a lost cut in a way (though, who really wants to see it?) Apparently this lost version was similar to the Danish version aside from excising the musical numbers (the flying scenes were still present at this point.) Sid Pink said, "AIP converted my version. My version doesn't exist anymore." [REPTILICUS - THE SCRIPT, pp.15]

So I doctored up *Reptilicus*. There were no close-ups, so we had to do some close-ups of objects, so we could have something to cut away from it. And I did some re-editing, and I put in a couple of extra scenes that we could do without the actors, and the end result was that AIP accepted the film and distributed it. [https://vantagepointinterviews.com/2017/05/18/the-imagination-of-ib-melchior-a-conversation-with-the-danish-monster-movie-maker]

AIP ultimately decided to cut out the now infamous scenes of the monster

flying, nor did the new dubbing script ever reference the creature's ability to fly. Instead, the U.S. version gave the monster its own unique power, the ability to spew a green slime from its mouth. (As such, this necessitated new dialogue to be looped in that was never in the shooting script.) The green slime also served as a way for the monster to greater menace the extras, as there seemed to be a disconnect between the monster and the fleeing humans, which never shared the same shot together.

In addition to cutting the shoddier shots, they also shortened shots of the

THE GERMAN REPTILICUS In addition to the Danish and English versions of REPTILICUS there was almost a third German version according to several sources. According to an article on actress Hanne Smyrner, entitled"Hanne's Big Ambitions" and appearing in the August 6, 1960 issue of BILLEDBLADET, the actress had to relearn her role in three languages! She also mentions that the Germans were unable to "partake in the great work." Likewise, the actor who played Svend (Bent Mejding) said that, "We did two versions: one in Danish and one in English. We also should have done a German version. But the German slipped out of it before the shooting started." Despite those two comments, producer Sid Pink ascertains that the film was only ever Danish and US coproduction.

monster that they did retain. To try and improve the footage of the monster that they kept, it was double-frame printed and slowed down. This added a sense of scale to the monster and the double-printing helped to hide some of the pesky wires. (This is why the U.S. version of *Reptilicus* has "grainy" footage of the monster that seems mismatched.) Smoke and fire burning in the background were also optically inserted into shots as well. Because they had little faith in the film and were on the cheap, AIP hired the Ray Mercer Company to do the optical printing. As the cheapest optical printers in the business, AIP got what they paid for.

Reptilicus was dubbed at Titra, which often handled Toho's Godzilla and special effects films. Furthermore, writer Ib Melchior also dubbed half a dozen characters according to his testimony!

The film was finally released in the U.S. in 1963, two years after its Danish premiere. Though poorly reviewed, the film still grossed around $800,000 in U.S., which was respectable for the time.

Amazingly, *Reptilicus* has managed to endure all these years, perhaps thanks to rather than in spite of the terrible puppet. It's actually possible that the movie would be less well-remembered if it had a good monster on screen!

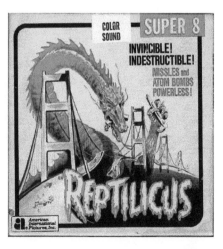

As far as we know, Ib Melchior's story for *Reptilicus* didn't change much in terms of the basic outline, but the monster's design/abilities definitely evolved along the way. Originally, Melchior envisioned Reptilicus as a "serpent with a bat's head," and later he described it as a combination between a sauropod-type dinosaur and a Pteranodon. As for the monster's wings, it's unknown who for sure added them (they may have been purely ornamental as far as Melchior was concerned), but it was Sid Pink's idea to make the monster fly. In Melchior's mind, it made sense for the monster to escape the lab and continue to grow in the canals of Copenhagen, where it would be confined to the city. Melchior told Brett Homenick:

I did not describe him as flying. Sid put that in. I like logic. I like things to be explained, and I want it to make sense. Now Reptilicus is confined to Copenhagen. He can't go anywhere else than Copenhagen. If he's there, he has to do what he does in Copenhagen because he's really trapped there. But if he could fly, he could fly anywhere he wanted! If they started shooting at him in Copenhagen, then he could fly down to Africa or whatever he wanted to do. So it didn't make sense to have him fly. [https://vantagepointinterviews.com/2017/05/18/the-imagination-of-ib-melchior-a-conversation-with-the-danish-monster-movie-maker]

Another thing that wasn't originally in the picture was the silly Peterson character, written specifically for Danish superstar Dirch Passer. Along with Passer came a few Danish musical numbers too. Of course, we could go on and on about the minute differences from script to screen concerning the dialogue and the "people parts," but you want to know about the discarded monster scenes, so here they are:

During the first confrontation with the military, there was to be a scene of Reptilicus chasing a soldier. The man, a machine gunner, abandons his post, and the monster slithers after him. Minus the shot direction, the script reads:

He is following the running soldier with his hideous head – Then he opens his mouth wide – and begins to lower his head towards the ground..... Far below the soldier is running – terror stricken; he stumbles, and falls; across him. Reptilicus is bending down; with his gigantic jaws he picks up the screaming man – and crushes him..... Like an enraged Terrier with a rat the monster shakes the lifeless body of the soldier – and flings it into the trees..... [pp. 47 of the script as reprinted in *Reptilicus – The Screenplay*]

Another exciting deleted scene occurs towards the end of the depth charge sequence. The scripts states:

Out of the swirling, bubbling water the hideous head of Reptilicus is rising... In front of the patrol boat the head and long neck of the monster rises out of the deep – looming over the boat..... Still nakedly hairless – still staring with blinded, scorched eyes – it crashes down on top of the boat with a deep roar, smashing it – and carrying the shattered pieces and the crew with it beneath the turbulent, seething water....! [Ibid, pp.58]

Notably it is at this point that the doctor has a heart attack at the sight of the accident.

As scripted, the flying scenes were also much more ambitious. When the monster flies over Hamburg, Germany, it was intended to land: "The big, ornate, German Renaissance City Hall building looms large in the F.G.......... Reptilicus comes flying towards it – and lands thunderously on its roof; one of the beast's huge wings strike the tower – shearing it off............ The tower topples – and crashes down on top of several other buildings...." [Ibid, pp.63]

The script describes several other

buildings tumbling down like dominoes and then returns to the monster who, on top of the building, flaps his wings and roars. Reptilicus takes off again as his tail and rear legs "hit and demolish some tall buildings nearby..." Reptilicus continues his flight through the city as various German soldiers fire upon him:

Reptilicus is flying low over the dock area; below can be seen the skeletal structures of the huge cranes and lifts........... A searchlight beam hits him square in the face – blinding him............ He throws his head back and bellows angrily; he makes a sharp turn in the air.......... Reptilicus momentarily blinded by the searchlight, crashes into one of the tall cranes..... He makes a heavy, destructive landing on the docks, tearing and ripping buildings and equipment alike. [Ibid, pp.64]

Some more destruction ensues, and the script states that with "a lumbering run" the monster takes off and flies away from the heart of the city.

Just as *Gorgo* had a deleted scene involving a circus elephant, here too Reptilicus was to scuffle with animals. The monster was to fly over a zoo where elephants would trumpet in horror which would in turn get all of the other animals to "roaring, shrieking, howling and trumpeting their fear... In a cacophony of bloodcurdling noise..." [Ibid]

Reptilicus answers the cries of the animals with a roar of his own then, "suddenly Reptilicus makes a swooping pass at the lion compound; with his huge, powerful rear legs he levels the moat that isolates the compound; his tail lashes out – felling trees and leveling small structures...." As such the lions escape to terrorize the people at the zoo as the monster flies away leaving the city in ruins. [Ibid, pp.63-66]

Later in the script, the monster's wings, which had been damaged in the previous scene, are described as simply skeletal remains which the monster flaps in a vain effort to fly. Among the more amusing deleted bits from the climactic city destruction was a sequence of a man who runs into a house of mirrors to seek shelter. As he tries to find a way out he only sees "grotesquely distorted images of himself..." Eventually the monster crushes the mirror house in what sounded to be a frightening scene. There was also to be a scene of a mother and young daughter taking refuge from the monster inside of an abandoned building which it passes by and destroys.

The monster was also supposed to single out and destroy a couple of machine gunners on a rooftop. Specifically, he was going to use his tiny arm to somehow knock them off the roof. The comically tiny arms come in to play again in the script, clearly written before the monster prop was created. The shot envisioned the monster seeing a big electric sign on one of the corners of the buildings. For some reason he becomes angry at it and "with his grotesque little forelimbs he rips the structure from the building hurtling it to the ground, as sparks and puffs of smoke crackle and explode from the shorted live wires."

After this, the screenplay plays out as in the finished film.

Above: Toho's two new Godzilla and Anguirus suits, created to fill in the blanks in THE VOLCANO MONSTERS. Though similar, they are not identical to the suits from GODZILLA RAIDS AGAIN, seen on the page opposite. Right: Mysterious photo of the VOL-CANO MONSTERS Godzilla suit pos-ing with the Phantom of the Opera!!!
GODZILLA RAIDS AGAIN © 1955 TOHO CO., LTD.

Like *Gorgo*, in a roundabout way, *Reptilicus* has roots in the Godzilla series. As it stands, many of *Reptilicus's* story elements and structure come from an unmade Godzilla film, or rather, an unproduced Americanization of an existing Godzilla film called *The Volcano Monsters...*

Godzilla Raids Again (1955) almost had what would surely have been one of the most notorious Americanizations in the series' history. Whereas *Godzilla, King of the Monsters!* (1956) merely edited Raymond Burr into the original *Godzilla, The Volcano Monsters* would have taken things a step further by completely eliminating the entire Japanese cast of *Godzilla Raids Again*! Not only that, Godzilla and Anguirus would be retrofitted to become a tyrannosaurus rex and an ankylosaurus, respectively, who run amuck in San Francisco's Chinatown!

This was orchestrated in part by Paul Schreibman, Harry Rybnick, Richard Kay, and Edmund Goldman, all of whom had a hand in the Americanized *Godzilla, King of the Monsters.* Ib Melchior, not yet the author of *The Angry Red Planet*, wrote *The Volcano Monsters* with Ed Watson revolving around Caucasian actors. An ad was even placed for the film in *Variety* in their May 7, 1957, issue with a starting date of June 17th.

Toho, eager to get a foothold in the American marketplace, agreed to the idea and, although the script meshed well with the actual footage, Toho ac-

tually constructed new suits of Godzilla and Anguirus to fill in the gaps of The Volcano Monsters script, and photos of these suits exist taken by Toho. Among the new scenes that would need to be filmed were the discovery of the dinosaurs, their trip across the ocean on a Navy Destroyer, and the Tyrannosaurus destroying a university building. (There are other mentions of the Navy bombing the monster similar to *Reptilicus*, but these scenes could have very well played out as exposition). Toho had already done something similar in the case of the American version of 1955's *Abominable Snowman*, which needed an additional scene to be filmed before it became the John Carradine vehicle *Half Human* in 1958. In this case, Toho sent the young Snowman suit to America for the filming of new scenes (though in the finished film, it's merely a corpse lying on a table).

It's worth noting that around this time a deal was struck with AB-PT Pictures

to help finance the film, which also (presumably) led Toho into working on the monster film that eventually became *Giant Monster Varan* (1958) with AB-PT. This division of the television network ABC that specialized in TV movies later collapsed in July of 1957, which meant the cancelation of *The Volcano Monsters*. As to what happened to the new Godzilla and Anguirus suits shipped to America, their fate is still a mystery. Blogger Ken Husley writes, "A few years ago I looked into the matter some and discovered that the old AB-PT studio property and structures became part of Desilu Studios, which then became part of the Paramount lot." In *Japanese Sci-*

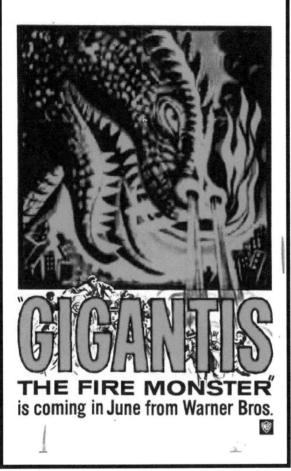

"GIGANTIS"
THE FIRE MONSTER"
is coming in June from Warner Bros.

the form of a remarkable color photo of the Godzilla suit posing with the Phantom of the Opera! Sources think it was taken at Universal Studios, though this has never been confirmed.

As to scripting, apparently, the writers weren't even aware that they were more or less adapting an existing film until late in the game. In an interview, Melchior said:

Ed and I were asked to... basically Americanize the Godzilla movies. I think the producers had seen the Japanese version of Gigantis, figured it would be released in the U.S., took the screenplay and said to Ed and I, 'Do this story.' Up until now, I had no idea that we might be redoing a Japanese script for an already completed movie.

ence Fiction, Fantasy and Horror Films Stuart Galbraith IV writes, "Markalite reported that effects man Bob Burns remembers seeing Gigantis and [sic] Angilas suits Toho presumably shipped to the United States for the new effects footage." This quote refers to Bob Burns during the shooting of 1957's Invasion of the Saucer Men. As he and the effects crew were preparing to blow up one of the alien saucers, they needed something to hide behind. They chose a large crate with curious Japanese writing on it. They opened it up to find the Godzilla and Anguirus suits, one of which Burns tried on.

Photographic evidence exists in

In another interview with Brett Homenick, Melchoir talked about the film's collapse:

Our final script was dated 5/7/1957 and was accepted by Rybnick, Barison, and Schreib-man. These three producers had a production/ distribution deal with a company called AB-PT when, in July of 1957, that company closed down. Now, for whatever reasons that I have no idea why, they did not replace the production/distribution company, and The Volcano Monsters bit the dust. I don't know if a copy of the script still exists somewhere. It's possible that I have it somewhere, but (laughs) I have no idea where.

After the collapse of *The Volcano Monsters*, Paul Schreibman, Edmund Goldman, and Newton P. Jacobs decided to merely dub *Godzilla Raids Again* into English and release it through Warner Bros with whom they had a distribution deal. Strangely, it was not billed as a Godzilla sequel even though *Godzilla, King of the Monsters!* had been an enormous hit in the United States. Back in the days before sequels were big business, Schreibman, Goldman, and Jacobs thought a new monster film would fare better and, as such, created the *Gigantis, the Fire Monster* name.

As to *The Volcano Monster's* complete script, it is par for the course when it comes to 1950s sci-fi in terms of its lead characters (Elderly scientist, check! Attractive female assistant, check! Chauvinistic military romantic lead, check!). At one point, the military hero, McBain, even punches the assistant, Marge, across the face to knock her out and rescue her from the Tyrannosaurus when she refuses to vacate her lab! However, that all being said, the duo of screenwriters did a commendable job of crafting a new storyline around the existing footage.

As stated earlier, some of Melchoir's ideas eventually found their way into *Reptilicus* (1961). First off, the main trope of characters is similar (but then again, aren't they always?) with the iron-jawed military man, an elderly scientist, and his attractive daughter (or daughters in *Reptilicus's* case). Said elderly scientist suffers a heart attack when he is unable to stop an attack on *Reptilicus* which would do the world more harm than good. As far as the idea of finding a preserved dinosaur, or in this case the preserved tail of a dinosaur-like creature, that was a fairly common convention by this time, but there is talk of the volcanic gasses preserving the dinosaurs in *Volcano Monsters*.

The other main similarity is that both scripts feature a scene where the female lab assistant makes some type of anti-monster biological weapon at a university when the monster is in close range. Then there are the depth charges used against the beast while its underwater. As in *Reptilicus*, there is both a threat of multiple monsters and also a plot point where the monster cannot be killed. In *Volcano Monsters*, killing the beast will make the main doctor character, recovering from a heart attack, spiral into death and depression if he can't study the beast (silly, we know). When the dinosaur, which is female, goes to an island to lay eggs, the threat of multiple monsters is introduced. *Volcano Monsters* ends with another dinosaur emerging from the volcano, and *Reptilicus* ends hinting that the titular monster will regenerate again.

So, in a strange roundabout way, *The Volcano Monsters* ended up influencing the writing process for the most famous Danish monster movie of all time: *Reptilicus!*

perfectly preserved, possibly by the volcanic gasses. When Carlyle plans to have the monsters transported to San Francisco, a Japanese resident warns him the dinosaurs, which he calls the "monsters of Noshiro," are the fulfilment of an ancient prophecy and will cause destruction if awakened. At a press conference in Tokyo, Carlyle explains that the two dinosaurs seem to be offshoots, or cousins, of the ankylosaurus and tyrannosaurus, perhaps explaining their larger than normal sizes. After this, the U.S. Navy dynamites the mouth of the cave to create a bigger opening to haul the behemoths through. They construct a gigantic bridge to an awaiting aircraft carrier on the shore of the Noshiro Volcano. The monsters are pulled on board via cables and prepared for their long voyage across the Pacific. During the voyage, Marge develops feelings for Navy commander Steve McBain, who is somewhat resentful of his assignment. Though McBain sometimes refers to her simply as "lady scientist," he also tells her, "How do you expect a guy to tell you how pretty you are and everything when you always change the subject to dinosaurs." Also on the voyage is another scientist named Corvin, who is resentful of the blossoming attraction between McBain and Marge. When it is learned the monsters are not only perfectly-preserved but also in a state of suspended animation, McBain wants to throw them overboard in fear they could awaken at any moment. When Corvin learns the monsters are alive, he fears that the cable on the tyrannosaurus is too tight and might damage it, and so he

After a huge eruption occurs at Noshiro volcano in Japan, a cavern is discovered containing perfect prehistoric stalactite and stalagmite formations. American paleontologist Dr. Roy Carlyle, along with his assistant Marge and some Japanese scientists survey the cave for fossils but find more than they bargained for in the form of two perfectly-preserved dinosaurs. Specifically, it is a male Ankylosaurus and a female Tyrannosaurus Rex that were presumably locked in battle when overtaken by the eruption. The two giant forms, several hundreds of feet long, seem to be dead but are loosens it. During a storm, the cable holding the Tyrannosaurus snaps and it tumbles across the deck, crushing a soldier, before falling into the water. The Ankylosaurus is delivered safely to San Francisco. In celebration, Marge and McBain go out on the town while at the same time the Tyrannosaurus surfaces in the bay. This disturbs the Ankylosaurus who breaks loose of its harness to battle its opponent. Their destruction causes a power outage, and also the driver of a CalTex truck gets frightened by the monster and crashes his vehicle into a refinery, starting a massive fire. Eventually, the monsters fight their way into Chinatown. A guilt-ridden Carlyle has a stroke and when Marge and McBain visit him in the hospital and he implores them to destroy the dinosaurs. However, Carlyle's doctor tells the duo that if this happens, Carlyle will lose his shot at the Nobel Prize and will likely become so depressed that he will die. Meanwhile, the Tyrannosaurus kills the Ankylosaurus by biting down on its neck. It then marches on through the mainland. Marge and a team of scientists work tirelessly at her university to make a recreation of the volcanic gas to put the dinosaur back to sleep. As the monster approaches their campus, McBain arrives to rescue Marge and when she refuses to leave, knocks her out with a punch to the face. McBain carries Marge to safety as the dinosaur destroys the building and then slips off into the sea, unphased by the military assault that escorts it out of the city. The Navy then attacks the Tyrannosaurus with bombs and depth charges to no avail. McBain and Marge follow the creature on a Navy destroyer into the Arctic, and eventually deduce it is heading for a tropical island in the polar region shielded by ice caps. Another scientist named Mitchel theorizes it is going there to lay eggs and warns that they'll soon have the dinosaur's brood to contend with. Though nuking the

monster is considered, a plan is hatched to bury the dinosaur in an avalanche. When the dinosaur comes ashore on the icy island, to trap the monster, the military places a ring of oil drums at the entrance to trap the beast. One of the men becomes trapped under one of the barrels and the monster approaches, and McBain must save him. As they run away, McBain tosses a grenade into the oil drum, igniting a ring of fire trapping the Tyrannosaurus. Jet fighters then bombard the canyon walls with rockets to induce the avalanche that buries the dinosaur. The plan works and Dr. Carlyle's prized possession is rendered harmless but still left alive in a state of suspended animation. Meanwhile, back at Noshiro Volcano, a claw bursts from the cave from an unknown monster...

Top Left: The Anklysaur discovered in the volcano. Middle: The T-Rex takes a dive from the carrier. Bottom Left: The T-Rex and the anklysaur duke it out in San Francisco! Above: The lady dinosaur prepares to lay her eggs on a secret Arctic Island. GODZILLA RAIDS AGAIN © 1955 TOHO CO., LTD.

Above: Cast photo featuring the Danish version of Connie (third from left) played by Bodil Miller. Inset: Danish poster for REPTILICUS. Next Page: Stills from the famous flying scene.

For many years, before the internet made things easier for lovers of rare films, western fans long bemoaned that the Danish cut of *Reptilicus* had extra monster footage. Specifically, most all sources acted as though the only ex-

tra monster footage comprised of the famous flying scene, but this is not the case. Not only does the Danish cut of *Reptilicus* contain more unique monster footage than just that, as it turns out, so does the AIP cut! Considering that both cuts had very little precise footage in common (as both filmed their own versions of each scene), an exhaustive study of the differences between the two versions will not be attempted in this article. Instead, we'll just hit the highlights.

The two cuts differ from the start, as the Danish version has credits that play over a serene landscape to like music.

AIP's version has only a few moments of this, just long enough to show the AIP logo for a few dramatic bars of music. This landscape footage is also narrated, telling us where we are, while the Danish version is not. Furthermore, when the flesh is discovered on the drill, the title, in blood dripping red letters, displays over Svend's bloody gloves. This is much better than Danish version which superimposed the title in rather bland font over the landscape footage. (The title placed over the bloody gloves is also how Melchior scripted it, so the Danish version deviated from his vision in that case.) The gore in the discovery is different too. The U.S. version utilizes closeups of the flesh caught on the drill, but the Danish version uses a longshot. The Danish cut also shows a brief shot of what looks to be a tiny Reptilicus foot in the wheel barrel, though it's hard to tell (whatever it is, it's not in the U.S. version).

Jumping ahead a bit, the U.S. version has some wide exterior shots of Copenhagen identifying it as such, while the Danish version does not. Most of the extra ten minutes worth of footage in the Danish version is dedicated to the relationship between the Martens sisters and Svend. There's a scene of the two sisters together in their room that isn't in AIP's version, which reveals to us that Lise is coming off of a bad breakup. There is also an extra scene of Svend and Karen on the beach together, where Svend seems frustrated.

There's also significant casting change we need to discuss before we go any further. The Connie Miller character is played by a different actress in both versions. The U.S. version of the character is blonde (Marlies Behrens) while

the other is dark-haired (Bodil Miller). Regarding Connie, after the reporters observe the creature in the tank for the first time, there's a short, heated exchange between General Grayson and Connie in the Danish version only. On the note of the tank, the U.S. version shows fluid circulating within it, while the Danish cut does not (this was likely new footage filmed by AIP in the States for the recut). The U.S. version follows the tank scene with a barrage of headlines, while the Danish version follows it with Professor Martens listening to a recording he made. It describes Reptilicus growing in a fetal position, and its bodily characteristics including the bat-like wings that the U.S. cut ignored. (This scene is in the U.S. version, but placed elsewhere and minus mention of the wings.) Martens' scene in the Danish cut is followed by another, happier beach scene between Svend and Karen, where they profess their love.

For the most part, the Danish version of *Reptilicus* is just fine up until the thirty minute mark. Up until this point, it's like watching the U.S. version from different angles and in a different language. But then comes the song and dance number... As Peterson sits outside reading the paper, he is suddenly surrounded by a group of children and they all break into song together about Reptilicus (shortened to 'Tilicus for the song)! It's truly bizarre tonally speaking. But, such scenes were common in Danish films back then, so for them it wouldn't have been odd apparently. On the note of Peterson, two of his comical scenes are compressed together for the U.S. cut, which features the scene of him eating a sandwich and playing with a microscope back to back with the electric eel scene. (The Danish cut splits those two scenes up.) In the infamous eel scene, Peterson cries for his mother in Danish, too.

In the U.S. version, following Peterson's scare, we get the scene of Professor Martens listening to his tape recorder that occurred earlier in the Danish cut. As the tape plays, here we get shots of the infantile Reptilicus, but they are so close up its difficult to know what we are looking at. Notably, Martens' narration includes mention of the corrosive slime added into AIP's version, and no mention of the wings.

After this, both versions feature a little travelogue sequence featuring the Tivoli Nights musical number. In both, Grayson takes Connie out on the town, though a different actress figures into each cut. The Danish version has some extra footage in this section of the film. After Peterson's microscope scene in the Danish version, we cut to Martens' country home, where the family and Svend are vacationing—nothing of any real consequence happens. (We do get a scene of Lise trying on dresses in a hope that she can steal Grayson away from Connie.) The sequence ends with Grayson and Connie driving up to the house for some social time, and we cut back to the lab. There, the Danish version lacks shots of the slimy Reptilicus stirring in its tank present in the AIP cut (again, that was likely new footage that Saga never had access to). The scene tries to play it for horror and laughs both, as we get suspenseful shots of Dr. Dalby getting a gun to check on the monster, and Peterson trying and failing to ride a bike in the rain. As for one last difference, both cuts have a shot of the monster rising up out of the lab, but both are different. The Danish version shows the silhouette of the wings, while the AIP version shows the neck. (Also, AIP inserted a shot of a downed telephone pole to further emphasize that the power was out during the scene.)

Reptilicus's big reveal in the country is different between the two cuts. In both versions we begin with the farmer standing by his dead cow and AIP's version follows this with the military fighting the monster right away. The Danish version goes to the scene where Reptilicus terrorizes a poor farming family in their country home first, a scene that takes place latter in AIP's version. Furthermore, AIP re-edits the scene to make it look as though Reptilicus eats the father, something he doesn't do in the Danish cut, which likewise includes a shot of what looks to be a full-scale foot prop crashing through the roof. At the end of the confrontation, as the charred monster slithers into the sea, Connie remarks about Reptilicus regenerating in both. But, in the Danish version, she says that maybe next time he'll use his wings.

For the underwater bombing scenes, the Danish version uses overhead long-shots of the monster, while AIP uses extreme close-ups.

And now onto the infamous flying scenes. Even if the effects are poorly done, the music and direction for the flying scenes are great and have a wonderful sense of urgency and momentum. (Considering the effects were pretty shoddy overall anyway, it's too bad AIP cut them.) There are about four brief flying shots, three at night, one in the day, and all mostly in a darkened profile. Instead of charting the monster's flight path, the U.S. version reports a trail of capsized ships at sea. When the monster emerges at the beach later, it slimes all the beachgoers, presumably killing them.

The ending, where Grayson fires the chemical rocket into the monster's mouth, uses different angles and shots. In the Danish version, we can see the rocket launcher in the same frame as the monster, but not so in the AIP cut. The music also seems to be different in both. Furthermore, Grayson ends up with different girls in each version. In the Danish version he ends the picture romantically involved with the doctor's daughter, Lise, while the U.S. version ends with he and Connie together. Lastly, the Danish version ends with an instrumental version of Tivoli Nights over a black end card with no text. The AIP cut ends with the same music, but with the credits against a blue background.

Which version is better? That's tough to say as both have their pros and cons. The AIP version wins in terms of Reptilicus's roar, which is better. The green slime is also pretty unique… but we don't get the flying scenes. If anything, I'd love to see a fan do a hybrid edit that excises the silly song and dance number from Peterson, but reinstates the flying scenes. Currently, the U.S. *Reptilicus* Blu-Ray is out of print, but here's hoping that a new release down the road will include both versions.

NOT SINCE **"KING KONG"** HAS THE SCREEN EXPLODED WITH SUCH MIGHTY FURY AND SPECTACLE!

AMERICAN-INTERNATIONAL PICTURES presents

K O N G A

IN COLOR AND SPECTAMATION

MICHAEL GOUGH · MARGO JOHNS · JESS CONRAD · CLAIRE GORDON

KONGA

Release Date: March 22, 1961

DIRECTED BY: John Lemont SPECIAL EFFECTS BY: Herman Cohen & Ronnie Whitehouse SCREENPLAY BY: Herman Cohen & Aben Kandel MUSIC BY: Gerard Schurmann CAST: Michael Gough (Dr. Charles Decker) Margo Johns (Margaret) Jess Conrad (Bob Kenton) Claire Gordon (Sandra Banks) Austin Trevor (Dean Foster) Suit Performers: Paul Stockman (Konga)

SpectaMation, Eastmancolor, 90 Minutes

SYNOPSIS After being presumed dead in Africa, Dr. Charles Decker returns to civilization one year later. With him are his precious pet chimp, Konga, and a bevy of carnivorous plants. Decker proves that the plants have a secret growth formula within them, which he injects into baby Konga. The ape soon grows larger with each injection, and Decker uses the giant chimp to murder his enemies and colleagues. Margaret, Decker's longtime assistant, blackmails Decker into proposing to her. However, Decker only has eyes for his student, Sandra. When Margaret catches Decker forcing himself on Sandra, she injects Konga with a final dose of the growth formula causing the ape to burst through the ceiling. Konga grabs Decker and walks through downtown London causing people to panic. Eventually, he is shot and killed by the military and Decker is killed when the ape throws him to the ground.

OVERVIEW: Perhaps the most famous of all the *King Kong* imitators is *Konga* for a number of reasons. The project began when producer Nathan Cohen asked Herman Cohen (no relation) to create for him another horror/exploitation film to follow *Horrors of the Black Museum*. In an interview with Tom Weaver, Herman Cohen stated, "Well, I had always flipped over *King Kong* and *Mighty Joe Young* and all that, so I came up with *Konga* and Aben Kandel and I started working on the script." Due to Cohen's past success with *I Was a Teenage Werewolf*, the company for a time called this film *I Was a Teenage Gorilla*! The film was a $500,000 co-production split equally between American International Pictures and Anglo Amalgamated. The former would distribute in America and the latter in Great Britain, where the film was set and filmed in Croydon, a large town in south London. Unlike the many *King Kong* imitators of the 1970s, Konga producer Herman Cohen actually approached RKO first and paid them $25,000 to use the King Kong name for "exploitation purposes." In a strange way, this makes *Konga* semi-legitimate in the annals of Kong related films.

Effects shooting took 18 months to complete, as it was one of the first

special effects films shot in color—relatively speaking at least. "*Konga* was in color and that's a whole different bag of beans. To have Konga hold Michael Gough, what I had to do there was matte five different scenes on one frame," Cohen said in an interview with Tom Weaver. Cohen worked closely with Rank Labs special effects director, Victor Marguetti, who developed a travelling matte process involving yellow sodium lights—the first picture this technique was ever used on. AIP reportedly didn't appreciate the lengthy process. "AIP was after me constantly," Cohen told Weaver. "'Where's the picture? When are we gonna get the picture?' They didn't realize how much work was involved..."

To bring Konga to life on a low budget, rather than build a new costume, George Barrow's famous gorilla suit used in *Gorilla at Large* and *Robot Monster* (1953) was used. Ever the showman, Cohen was also quite proud of the giant carnivorous plants created for the film. "My art director Wilfred Ar-

nold and I did a lot of research on those plants. I had to go to all kinds of places with him...They were based on actual carnivorous plants. We had them made at Sheperton Studios."

One of the trickiest aspects of shooting was actually the on-location shots for Konga's climax. Cohen was warned by both his production managers, Jim

O'Connolly and Jack Greenwood, that the Metropolitan Police would never give him permission to shoot on the streets. And, unlike America, they warned him that English policemen weren't so easy to bribe. Undeterred, Cohen went to see the inspector in charge of Croydon. Rather than pester him to death, Cohen sat and listened to the inspector, and the two conversed about multiple subjects. When the inspector mentioned he wished that he could afford a color television set, Cohen had one sent to his home soon after. Cohen was then granted permission to shoot on the streets of Croydon from midnight to 5AM for five nights. Cohen told Weaver, "The thing that I didn't mention to him was that, at the finale, all hell was going to break loose—that we were going to shoot sub-machine guns, bazookas, etc., etc."

The aforementioned scene Cohen purposely didn't shoot until the very last night, naturally. Though the inspector had stayed away from the set all the other nights, on the final night he stopped by for a friendly visit to Cohen's horror. Cohen told his crew to have their trucks running and ready to go, because once they shot the gunfire scenes they may need to leave quickly. And indeed, when the gunfire sequences began England's 999 emergency number received over 300 phone calls! The police later gave Cohen the names of over twenty people who were threatening to go to the Consul over the incident. Cohen and his producers bought expensive chocolates and flowers and went to see the complainers one by one! Remarkably, Cohen stayed out of legal trouble.

As to the finished film, in essence, one could consider the first half an update of *Murders of the Rue Morgue* and the climax an inferior version of *King Kong*—not to mention that the idea of a scientist using a growth serum on a chimpanzee originated in an earlier Cohen film, *Bela Lugosi Meets a Brooklyn Gorilla* (1952). Sadly there's really not much of interest going on in *Konga's* finale. The large ape grows to giant size, picks up Michael Gough, and begins walking around London until he is shot to death in front of Big Ben. The only miniature destroyed is Gough's home.

More people seem to remember the film for Gough's performance. The actor returned from Cohen's *Horrors of the Black Museum* and more or less carries *Konga*—not an easy feat with the goofy ape suit running around. Hammer alum Gough's character seems to be right out of a Hammer film, considering he is selfish, violent, and won't hesitate to eliminate anyone who gets in his way. Actually, Gough's character is not unlike Peter Cushing's ruthless interpretation of Baron Frankenstein. With all the people Decker murders, not to mention complications brought on by an unwanted fiancé, the narrative is somewhat similar to Hammer's 1957 *Curse of Frankenstein*. There are other Hammer similarities as well. *Konga's* killing of the man in his study and the way he breaks through the glass brings to mind Hammer's *The Mummy* (1959). Coincidentally, *The Mummy's* George Pastell is then *Konga's* next victim! The fact that nearly all of the main characters die—including sympathetic ones like Sandra (chomped on by one of the plants)—makes *Konga* something of a hard-boiled film with a goofy looking title character.

Unfortunately, not much is known of *Konga's* early, discarded story concepts—assuming it even had any. Perhaps it went through very little development? Maybe the story was always as simple as a chimpanzee getting injected with a growth formula and enlarging itself to terrifying heights? It could be, but considering that the film's original title was *I Was a Teenage Gorilla*, is it possible that it started out with a somewhat different storyline?

As stated before, Herman Cohen was the producer of a trilogy of famous "I Was a Teenage [fill-in the blank]" series in the late 1950s. In fact, *I Was a Teenage Werewolf* (1958) helped to put American International Pictures on the map when it came to teenage horror films. That film's success quickly encouraged two sequels later that same year, *I Was a Teenage Frankenstein* (self explanatory) and *Blood of Dracula*. (The latter should have been called *I Was a Teenage Vampire*, but for whatever reason wasn't.) Due to the success of the two sequels Roger Corman changed the title of his upcoming caveman film from *The Prehistoric World* to *Teenage*

Caveman. Likewise, the original title for AIP's *Attack of the Puppet People* (1958) was *I Was a Teenage Doll*!

Cohen's three "I Was a Teenage..." flicks all had one thing in common: an older scientist performing experiments on a teenager that turns them into a monster. Could we presume then that *I Was a Teenage Gorilla* had the same story structure? Let's take a look at *Konga's* story again. Dr. Dekker does teach college students. What if in the original version, Dekker turned Sandra's boyfriend Bob into a gorilla? Maybe he didn't even grow gigantic in the end? This is just my own speculation running wild though.

Cohen had actually already done a storyline very similar to what I just speculated in the form of *Bela Lugosi Meets a Brooklyn Gorilla* (1952) in the film. Dr. Zabor (Lugosi) is conducting 'evolutionary' experiments on gorillas and chimpanzees via growth serum. Sadly none of the apes grow to Kong-size as in *Konga*. Instead, Dr. Zabor's serum reverses the evolutionary process, turning a chimp into a monkey(!), and later reverts Duke Mitchell into the titular Brooklyn Gorilla.

Or, perhaps, Konga the chimp was always the "Teenage Gorilla" of the abandoned title? Konga is a baby at the start of the film, and perhaps one could consider his gorilla form to be the ape as a teenager? Until confirmation comes along, we can keep on wondering...

Though *Gorgo* fans have long lamented the fact that the monstrous mother and son never got a big screen sequel, they did get a follow-up comic book series by Charlton Comics that ran from 1961 into 1965. The first issue faithfully adapted the film and even included an ambitious deleted scene that didn't make it into the movie. Since Gorgo and Ogra both survived the picture's end, crafting a sequel story wasn't difficult.

The sequel story, "The Return of Gorgo", is essentially just a retread of the first film where baby Gorgo wanders ashore in New York and causes destruction. Ogra comes to fetch him and joins in the mayhem. The issue ends with the monsters knocked out with a special gas and floating out to sea. After this, the creatures went on to have run-ins once an issue with either invading aliens, communists, or other giant monsters. One issue saw Gorgo and Ogra fight aliens in Melbourne, Australia (notable since *Gorgo* was almost set in Australia). Remarkably, Reptisaurus (Charlton's version of Reptilicus) showed up in one issue of Gorgo to help him destroy some flying saucers during another alien invasion. Sadly, that was the extent of the team-up, which really wasn't even a team-up and it's a wonder why Charlton never did Gorgo vs. Reptisaurus (or Konga for that matter).

Despite Reptisaurus's fleeting guest appearance, Charlton didn't have a strong sense of continuity with *Gorgo*. Or, that is to say, unlike the *Konga* comic, which featured reoccurring protagonists (occasionally at least), *Gorgo* focused solely on the monsters, with guest stars popping up each issue in terms of the human cast (a character might see a rare repeat performance, but they were of little significance).

The final issue would seem to qualify as a decent series finale in the form of *Gorgo* #23 ("Land of Long Ago", September 1965). In it, a scientist with a soft spot for Gorgo sends the dinosaur back in time to the Jurassic. (For some odd reason he doesn't take Ogra though!) The scientist accidentally goes back in time with Gorgo, and the monster must defend him from various dinosaurs. Eventually the duo begin jumping forwards in time until they land in the Ice Age, and then finally back in the present. In the last panels, the military vows to let baby Gorgo be and to stop pestering him from then on, having grown fond of him.

AND SO, BACK WITH HIS MASSIVE PARENT, GORGO RESTED AFTER HIS MIGHTY LABORS! TO SLEEP PERHAPS A YEAR--OR A CENTURY--OR FOREVER AS WE MEASURE TIME! FOR GORGO WAS BORN 2,000,000 YEARS AGO--AND HE'S YOUNG YET!

END

If the *Konga* movie failed to meet your expectations, the sequel comic book series might be more up your alley. Whereas *Gorgo's* motion picture had at least delivered on the monster action, *Konga's* movie was a let down for many giant monster fans. But fear not, in the case of the comic book, Konga, or rather Konga the second, gets up to all sorts of monster mayhem.

The first *Konga* special was an adaptation of the film with a few alterations. (Dekker didn't force Konga to kill: the ape's new psychic powers enabled him to hear Dekker's angry thoughts, which he carried out on his master's behalf.) The main alteration that affected Charlton's series was that Bob and Sandra survived the comic book version, unlike the film.

In "The Return of Konga", the two become the primary human protagonists of the series. When Bob finds some of Dekker's leftover growth serum, he can't resist injecting it into Sandra's new pet monkey, which she has named Konga in honor of the one that died. That Konga too grows into a giant gorilla, and all sorts of adventures are had by the trio. The main continuity thread is that Sandra and Bob, now a married couple, feel guilty for making Konga gigantic, and Bob does his best to come up with a cure for the big ape. The characters didn't feature into every issue, though. For some tales they were absent.

The series fell into one of three storylines where the giant ape either fought aliens, communists, or other giant monsters. One of the more interesting deviations took a page from *Gorgo* and *King Kong*, with Konga being captured by a circus and put on display as the 8th Wonder of the World! Another storyline preceded *King Kong Lives* (1986) and saw Konga finding a female giant ape!

The series main story-thread—curing Konga—was left unresolved. The final issue, *Konga* #23 (November 1965), saw the big ape in a knock-down drag-out fight with a dinosaur monster which, although satisfying, didn't resolve the big ape's story. (Considering that Sandra and Bob don't even show up, presumably Charlton didn't anticipate this being the final issue.) For all we know, Konga remained gigantic for the rest of his life.

The third and oddest of Charlton's little monster franchise was *Reptilicus*, which received the standard movie adaptation followed by a sequel. *Reptilicus* #2 ("In the African Jungle", October 1961) finds the monster's severed foot/fetus washing ashore in Africa. The regenerated Reptilicus terrorizes some natives, plus a visiting scientist and his daughter. Oddly, Reptilicus #2 is killed at the end of the issue via sinking into poisonous quicksand! Why exactly Charlton killed the monster after only two issues is unknown. It's presumed they may have only paid licensing fees for two issues, though Reptilicus creator Sid Pink ascertains that Charlton never paid for a license to begin with. Whatever the case, the series continued under the rebrand of *Reptisaurus the Terrible*.

Seeming to take inspiration from Rodan, the series focused on a male and female Reptisaurus which had become sealed within a volcano in prehistoric times. The dino-monsters are subsequently reawakened by the H-Bomb in the modern era. Right off the bat they make heroes of themselves by saving Earth from aliens from Jupiter. Oddly enough, issue #4 retconned this origin story right away, to make the millennia long mates strangers that have just met! Or, in other words, it was a monster love story predating *King Kong Lives* only with flying snakes.

The next issue then found Reptisaurus forgetting about his mate and falling in love with a mechanical dragon built by the Chinese communist party! The series improved with "Reptisaurus Returns" (the seventh and final regular issue, as it turned out), which gave the male and female monsters makeovers. The male became more anthropomorphic with more developed arms and legs (plus a horn on his snout) while the female looked more like a pterodactyl. The story saw the monster mates fly to Africa to raise up a new brood of little Reptisauruses. The story sadly ends

with the hatchlings killed in an atomic blast, though the parents survive. After this came a bonus issue, christened *Reptisaurus the Terrible Special Edition* #1 which saw the beast fly to Mexico where he is mistaken for Quetzalcoatl.

CHARLTON COMICS GIVE YOU MORE!
REPTILICUS
IN THE AFRICAN JUNGLE

FROM THE NORTH HE CAME, BORN ON ROARING WINGS THAT CARRIED HIM AT SPEED OF SOUND...A FLYING REPTILE WITH A HATRED OF ALL MANKIND, AN REDICTABLE, DEADLY ENEMY OF THE ENTIRE WORLD! MODERN MAN'S WEAPONS FAILED...AND THE PRIMITIVE INCANTATIONS OF THE WITCH DOCTOR PROVED LLY USELESS AGAINST REPTILICUS, THE TERRIFYING THROWBACK THAT GED FROM THE TIMELESS FROZEN MUCK OF LAPLAND, AND HAD BEEN A VERSAL NIGHTMARE EVER SINCE!

The Gripping Story Of A City Threatened With Annihilation By A Raging Prehistoric Monster

MM603
MONARCH
BOOKS
35¢

MONARCH
MOVIE
BOOK

GORGO

Carson Bingham

This classic thriller is now on the screen as a spectacular King Brothers' Technicolor Production

In 1960, Monarch Books published licensed adaptations of all three of the films that this issue is devoted to. Most of them also came out before the films were released, and let me tell you, if I were a kid in the 1960s and my mother read the books inspired by the films, she most likely would not have let me see said films! Monarch had their authors take the films' basic storylines and inject them

with a great deal of sex. While this wasn't too hard to do with *Konga* and *Reptilicus*, *Gorgo* was a challenge as it featured no female characters to begin with. As such, author Bruce Cassiday (using the pseudonym Carson Bingham) created a brand new character that was integral to the story: Moira McCartin. Ingeniously, she was made to be little orphan Sean's half-sister who also becomes Sam Slade's love interest. While originally it was little Sean who related most of the exposition regarding Gorgo and Ogra, here it is Moira, who acts as though the monster will bring about the apocalypse.

Aside from the apocalyptic subplot, there are some other interesting differences worth discussing. After Gorgo is brought to London, Professor Flaherty has concerns that the animal may be carrying unknown parasites or diseases (this was probably inspired by *The Beast from 20,000 Fathoms*). The film had a notable planned but deleted scene where the baby Gorgo was to tussle with an elephant. The book includes the scene, which is kicked off when flashbulbs from a reporter's camera sets the monster off à la *King Kong*. It's probably for the best that the scene was cut, as it's rather gory and features Gorgo killing the elephant, which makes him less sympathetic even if he is just an animal.

Upon hearing the news that the specimen that they captured was a baby, Slade returns to Nara Island. As such Slade is present when mama Ogra comes ashore. And guess what he's doing when she does? He's making love to Moira, of course. In another *Beast/Foghorn*-inspired scene, as Ogra surfaces she destroys a lighthouse.

MONSTER ON THE LOOSE

Sam Slade didn't believe in Gorgo until he saw the monster's hideous scaly face, its slimy green talons and the massive mouth that could swallow a killer whale.

Sam didn't believe in love, either, until he met virginal Moira McCartin and helped her to discover the deep passions slumbering within her.

Moira taught him to love and Gorgo taught him to fear. Spewn from some sub-oceanic cavern, the monster catapulted from the sea, threatening death for all who challenged it.

Captured, it presented even more of a problem, for deep in the bowels of the sea was a larger, more vicious monster, even now rising from the depths to rescue its offspring and to destroy everything in its path — battleships, tanks and half of London!

Published by MONARCH BOOKS, INC.

A terrifying scene from the King Brothers' Technicolor Movie

After that she trounces the village as she does in the film.

The city destruction sequences hit the same beats as the film with a few extras: Ogra snatches a fighter plane out of the sky, and tipping its hat to *King Kong* and *Godzilla*, the novel has Ogra destroy an oncoming train at one point. When mother and child return to the sea, Moira summarizes the whole incident by stating, "This visitation must be heeded, or there will be worse to come." Slade the replies, "H-Bombs. A-Bombs. Infinity. Space exploration. Unlocking the secret of life. I wondered if mankind would heed the warning. I doubted it. Man has a way of facing up to even the toughest challenges of the universe—and of life itself."

The *Gorgo* novelization was published in July 1960, nine months before the film's release in the U.S. Today it has been reprinted by Bear Manor Media if you'd like to give it a read.

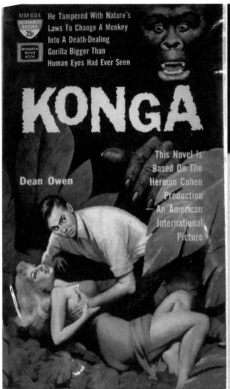

KONGA

Professor Decker's whole life was a series of evil secrets: There was his secretary, Margaret, who performed her official duties by day and her extra-curricular duties by night.

There was the secret of his potent new serum, which was changing the tiny monkey, Konga, into a gargantuan king gorilla. And there were the carnivorous jungle plants which could be grown large enough to swallow a man whole.

Blonde coed Sandra, eager to learn in or out of class, started as a secret, too. But when Decker's jealous lust for her and his fury at a rival scientist's discoveries drove him to murder, he used Konga as his instrument of destruction.

A Herman Cohen Production —
An American International Picture

Published By MONARCH BOOKS, INC.

While the kind-hearted *Gorgo* may have seemed unbefitting of such raunchy, hard boiled treatment, *Konga* was another story as it featured a thoroughly unlikable lead character and it had plenty of opportunities for sex, which author Dean Owen ran with.

In the novel, when Margaret finds out about Dekker's affair with Sandra, she decides in turn to have an affair with Sandra's boyfriend Bob! The death scenes are also more explicit, with Dekker watching Konga kill the Dean. In Professor Tagore's case, Konga beheads him!

And whereas Bob is killed in the driveway outside his home in the movie, in the book he is killed in Dekker's greenhouse. There Bob confronts his professor before Konga kills him. Sandra gets the worst of it. Though she's left for dead in the film, we don't know for sure that she died (she could have gotten away). In the book, Dekker rapes her and then she's graphically eaten by the giant carnivorous plants!

And though the book had an unlimited budget (so to speak) unlike the film, it still skimps on the giant Konga action. If anything, it seems like Dean Owen realizes he's written enough pages to satisfy the publisher and just wants to end it already!

Described as the weakest of the three Monarch adaptations, *Konga* may not be worth your time like *Gorgo's* novelization.

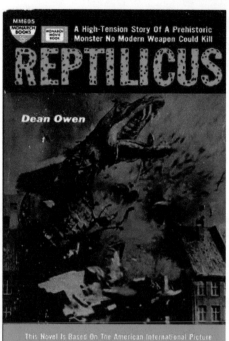

MM605

MONARCH BOOKS 35¢

A High-Tension Story Of A Prehistoric Monster No Modern Weapon Could Kill

REPTILICUS

Dean Owen

This Novel Is Based On The American International Picture

SPAWN OF HELL

A dramatic scene from the American International Picture

Reptilicus, the gargantuan prehistoric monster, crouched on the ocean bottom, ready to take off on another destructive rampage. A depth charge thundered. One of the beast's legs ripped from the body and was blown out of the sea. General Grayson looked at the girl beside him, wondering if he would live to enjoy Connie's warm, vibrant flesh again. Svend Alstrup, his aide, was remembering Karen's wanton seduction of him and hoping for a repeat performance.

Suddenly, Grayson panicked, realizing that if they blew the animal to pieces, each section could grow into a new monster. That was the ultimate danger — a whole new generation of giant, reptilian monstrosities roaming the earth and annihilating civilization.

He gave the order to cease firing . . .

SEE THE MOVIE — READ THE BOOK

Published By MONARCH BOOKS, INC.

Also written by Dean Owen, the *Reptilicus* novel begins with a steamy sex scene between Svend and his foreman's wife! Not exactly the same as the wholesome character from the film.

There's also some competition between Dr. Dalby and Professor Martens, as the former already has a Nobel Prize and Martens hopes the regenerating reptile can do the same for him.

It's quite clear that Owen wrote the book based off of the script, as his first description of Reptilicus reads just like the one in the script. This is further evidenced by the novel containing many scenes deleted from the film, such as the monster attacking a boat after the depth charge scene. The aerial attack on Hamburg is also included.

A scene not present in the script or the film takes place in the novel, where Grayson instigates a second flamethrower attack on the monster that burns through the membranes of its wings, grounding Reptilicus.

Notably, the film never explained how Reptilicus would be done away with once he was knocked out. Here, the soldiers pry the armored scales from the unconscious monster and the flamethrowers are able to burn the body into ash. So, if you ever wondered how they did away with the monster, that was it.

Due to the sleazy nature of the book, Sid Pink sued Monarch for "such lewd, lascivious and wanton desire as to inflame unsavory and lascivious desires in the reader".

After the financial success and hype generated by the 1998 GODZILLA remake, Sid Pink pondered taking Reptilicus out of retirement for either a remake or a sequel (sources aren't sure which). Pink announced the project in conjunction with Sam Sherman in 2001. The plan was to shoot the movie in Florida and bring Reptilicus to life with CGI. Pink got as far as hiring Gary Dohanish to create a new CGI Reptilicus model (pictured on page opposite). Sadly Pink passed away in 2002, and the project died with him.

This back to back double feature of GORGO and KONGA (advertised to the left) intentionally mislead children to believe they were watching an all new movie!

GORGO received a quasi-sequel in the form of the short comedy, WAITING FOR GORGO, running at 18 minutes and released in 2010. It's a well-produced, charming little film that doesn't feature the monster itself, only photographs. It centers around an audit of the Department of Monsters and Oversized Animals (DMOA). For a time, it seems that there's been a mix-up, and that the department was created when someone mistakenly took the film GORGO to be a real event. However, in the last scene, a member of the DMOA produces a gigantic tooth belonging to the real monster.

GORGO VS. GODZILLA? In the late 1960s, John Carpenter (HALLOWEEN) created a "Godzilla vs. Gorgo" fan film, which is probably as close as we're ever going to get to seeing the two titans battle on screen. Unfortunately, the short fan film has never been revealed to the public.

GIL GERARD

REPTISAURUS

As covered previously, early into Charlton Comic's *Reptilicus* series they rechristened the monster Reptisaurus, and a few issues after that, also tweaked the design a bit. As the Charlton Comics have themselves fallen into public domain, this has led some to think that both Reptilicus/Reptisaurus and Konga are fair game for unlicensed sequels and remakes. (People are leerier of Gorgo, perhaps because it's a more popular property than the other two.) While 2020's *Konga TNT* is a bit more brazen, back in 2009, Vision Films Inc. took a safer route in basing a movie on *Reptisaurus the Terrible*. At least, they say the movie is based on the comics, but I wonder about that. What little I can find on this film says that it started off with the title of *Sky Fighter*. I halfway wonder if someone decided that since the movie had a flying dragon in it, why not find a public domain character to base it off of? However, the opening credits do state that the film was based upon *Rept-*

isaurus the Terrible (but they could've tacked that on at the last second).

That said, does the movie have any similarities to the comic? Well, for starters it basically retcons Reptisaurus's origin as a prehistoric survivor into a genetically engineered creation, specifically a combination of a reptile and a bat. (This is interesting, as Reptilicus was described by Ib Melchior as being like a combination between a snake and a bat, so there's that connection at least.) This version of Reptisaurus is notably smaller than its comic book counterpart, though. The design isn't exactly spot on either with any of Reptisaurus's comic book forms (there were about three in all, four if you count Mrs. Reptisaurus). Next, you might ask if there is any commonality with the comic storylines at least? Eh, not really. On the one hand, a group of shipwrecked survivors stuck on an island with the monster sounds vaguely like one of the comics, but if it had been a comic story then Reptisaurus probably would have saved them from another monster. Instead, the monster spends the movie tearing the castaways to shreds.

Nor does the movie skimp on the monster's screen time. In fact, Reptisaurus shows up in the first scene. So at least the movie lets you know what kind of effects to expect upfront, which for a 2009 Syfy TV movie really aren't terrible. (But then again, are Asylum-budget CGI effects ever really that good?) Right away the monster attacks some fighter jets, and then on the island kills a man by pecking him to death (probably cheaper to animate that way). The movie's real story begins three months later, when some spring-breakers wash ashore on the island due to drunk boating. They meet up with two military officers sent to tag the animal so that it can be locked onto by high grade weaponry and destroyed.

Though that doesn't sound too awful, to be blunt, the movie is boring. To make matters worse, it's padded out *Planet of Dinosaurs* style, with long scenes of the survivors trekking through the dense island (which looks just like rural Los Angeles, naturally). It was pretty arduous to get through, and I found myself mostly waiting for them to get to the abandoned lab to see if the monster's origin had anything in common with Reptilicus or Reptisaurus, which it didn't (being genetically engineered and all). On that note, another monster pops up in flashback in the form of a genetically modified earthworm. Its brought to life with solid practical effects and eats a guy. These practical effects are good overall, but are used fleetingly. Most of the effects are dominated by the video-game quality Reptisaurus. (One source I found said that the monster was actually a Wyvern 2.0 model sold by DAZ 3D for $14.95!) The monster's scenes easily become repetitive, too, with the characters shooting at it over and over again while it roars at them or flies overhead. At the end, the military hero throws a stick of dynamite into its mouth and the monster's head explodes. But, like Reptilicus, it ends with the threat of another monster in the form of a nest of unhatched eggs.

(That's one thing it had in common with the comics at least: Reptisaurus eggs!)

Despite the almost in-name-only connection to Reptisaurus, today the film is better remembered for the fact that it starred Gil Gerard (*Buck Rogers*) and was directed by Christopher Ray, who has gone on to become of the main talents at The Asylum. Currently, the film is only available on DVD in Japan and Thailand, though it occasionally pops up on YouTube.

is better than Reptisaurus. My friend (Danny Lee Beane of *Beware! The Blob* article fame in this fanzine) told me the movie was basically a guy in a Halloween costume running around in front of a camcorder. And while this is basically true, it's at least aware of the fact that it's a guy in a Halloween costume in front of a camcorder (a good camcorder, by the way).

To get some assumptions out of the way about the movie's story, no it's not played as a sequel to the original 1961 *Konga* as there are no references to characters or events from that film. The film does at least have a few elements from the comics, which is more than I could say for *Reptisau-*

As I often say in my editorials, Coivd-19 boredom helped birth The Lost Films Fanzine. It also birthed a new movie: Konga TNT. Using the public domain Charlton Comics Konga series as a springboard, director Brett Kelly took some leftover/unused footage from his past films, shot some new footage (on virtually no budget, I assume) and created *Konga TNT*.

To my great surprise, I enjoyed *Konga TNT*. However, my expectations were pretty low. I was also just coming off of watching *Reptisaurus*, and anything

rus. As in the comics (and the original *Konga*), the title character starts off as a baby ape which grows into something gigantic. Sometimes the comics would have Konga revert to his original size, and that's also how this movie ends, but I'm getting ahead of myself.

Konga TNT begins with a flashforward of some jet fighters encountering the big ape. At first, I was worried the film was going to play it straight, as the pre-credit sequence I just mentioned is played seriously. After the credits finish, it's clear that the movie is a spoof. Sort of like *A*P*E* (1976), which also featured a Halloween quality ape suit. (A scene of Konga interacting with a kite especially seems like a callback to *A*P*E*.)

As the movie continues, we get some out of place footage of an alien craft crashing on Earth, this is followed by an Indiana Jones type vignette with an explorer out to capture the alien artifact. It's all a bit out of place and confusing, but I assume this was probably the leftover footage that Kelly had laying around. I thought that perhaps Konga would fight some aliens as he did in the comics, but instead the alien aspect simply ties into the ape's origin. A scientist uses the alien artifact recovered to somehow create a miracle serum called TNT which he tests on a plant (a callback to the original Konga) and then the tiny baby ape. (No real apes were used and I don't blame them, chimps can be mean!) Konga (a tiny puppet) is injected with the serum, escapes the lab, and befriends two young suburban brothers before succumbing to gigantism.

The giant Konga experiences his big growth spurt in a barn and he bursts through the roof in a nice nod to the original Konga. There is no miniature work, and instead Konga is integrated into real archive footage of buildings collapsing. All in all, it delivers the monster monkey action that you expected from the original, which was rather short on scenes of the giant Konga. Here, Konga spends nearly half the movie as a giant monster, which is something at least. It ends with a military confronta-

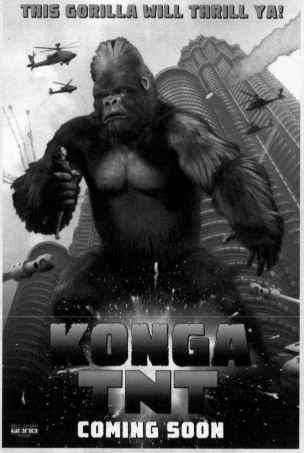

tion which again brings to mind *A*P*E* and the giant Konga suddenly shrinks back to size and reunites with the two brothers for a happy ending.

Like so many post-*Iron Man* movies, it even ends with a post-credits scene! In it, the two boys find a mysterious egg... and that's it. There's no dialogue to hint at what it might be, but I presume it probably belongs to Reptisaurus, the other public domain Charlton property.

Konga TNT is available through our friends at SRS Cinema, and as long as your expectations aren't too high (I would say to expect something just above a fan film) you might enjoy *Konga TNT*.

THE BICEP BOOKS CATALOGUE

The following titles are available for purchase on Amazon.com, and are available to bookstores at a wholesale discount via Ingram Content Group (ISBNs of available editions listed for this purpose)

THE BIG BOOK OF JAPANESE GIANT MONSTER MOVIES SERIES

The third edition of the book that started it all! Reviews over 100 tokusatsu films between 1954 and 1988. All the Godzilla, Gamera, and Daimajin movies made during the Showa era are covered plus lesser known fare like *Invisible Man vs. The Human Fly* (1957) and *Conflagration* (1975). Softcover (380 pp/5.83" X 8.27") Suggested Retail: $19.99 SBN:978-1-7341546-4-1

This third edition reviews over 75 tokusatsu films between 1989 and 2019. All the Godzilla, Gamera, and Ultraman movies made during the Heisei era are covered plus independent films like *Reigo, King of the Sea Monsters* (2005), *Demeking, the Sea Monster* (2009) and *Attack of the Giant Teacher* (2019)! Softcover (260 pp/5.83" X 8.27") Suggested Retail: $19.99 ISBN: 978-1- 7347816-4-9

This second edition of the Rondo Award nominated book covers un-produced scripts like *Bride of Godzilla* (1955), partially shot movies like *Giant Horde Beast Nezura* (1963), and banned films like *Prophecies of Nostradamus* (1974), plus hundreds of other lost productions. Softcover/Hard-cover (470pp. /7" X 10") Suggested Retail: $24.99 (sc)/$39.95(hc)ISBN: 978-1-73 41546-0-3 (hc)

This sequel to *The Lost Films* covers the non-giant monster unmade movie scripts from Japan such as *Frankenstein vs. the Human Vapor* (1963), *After Japan Sinks* (1974-76), plus lost movies like *Fearful Attack of the Flying Saucers* (1956) and *Venus Flytrap* (1968). Hardcover (200 pp/5.83" X 8.27")/Softcover (216 pp/ 5.5" X 8.5") Suggested Retail: $9.99 (sc)/$24.99(hc)   ISBN:978-1-7341546 -3-4 (hc)

This companion book to *The Lost Films* charts the development of all the prominent Japanese monster movies including discarded screenplays, story ideas, and deleted scenes. Also includes bios for writers like Shinichi Sekizawa, Niisan Takahashi and many others. Comprehensive script listing and appendices as well. Hardcover/Softcover (370 pp./ 6"X9") Suggested Retail: $16.95(sc)/$34.99(hc)ISBN: 978-1-7341546-5-8 (hc)

Examines the differences between the U.S. and Japanese versions of over 50 different tokusatsu films like *Gojira* (1954)/*Godzilla, King of the Monsters!* (1956), *Gamera* (1965)/*Gammera, the Invincible* (1966), *Submersion of Japan* (1973)/*Tidal Wave* (1975), and many, many more! Softcover (540 pp./ 6"X9") Suggested Retail: $22.99(sc)   ISBN: 978-1- 953221-77-3

This second volume examines the differences between the European and Japanese versions of tokusatsu films including the infamous "Cozzilla" colorized version of *Godzilla, King of the Monsters!* from 1977, plus rarities like *Terremoto 10 Grado*, the Italian cut of *Legend of Dinosaurs*. The book also examines the condensed Champion Matsuri edits of Toho's effects films. Coming 2022.

Throughout the 1960s and 1970s the Italian film industry cranked out over 600 "Spaghetti Westerns" and for every *Fistful of Dollars* were a dozen pale imitations, some of them hilarious. Many of these lesser known Spaghettis are available in bargain bin DVD packs and stream for free online. If ever you've wondered which are worth your time and which aren't, this is the book for you. Softcover (160pp./5.06" X 7.8") Suggested Retail: $9.99

THE BICEP BOOKS CATALOGUE

CLASSIC MONSTERS SERIES

Kong Unmade explores unproduced scripts like *King Kong vs. Frankenstein* (1958), unfinished films like *The Lost Island* (1934), and lost movies like *King Kong Appears in Edo* (1938). As a bonus, all the Kong rip-offs like *Konga* (1961) and *Queen Kong* (1976) are reviewed. Hardcover (350 pp/5.83" X 8.27")/Softcover (376 pp/ 5.5" X 8.5") Suggested Retail: $24.99 (hc)/$19.99(sc) ISBN: 978-1-7341546-2-7(hc)

Jaws Unmade explores unproduced scripts like *Jaws 3, People 0* (1979), abandoned ideas like a Quint prequel, and even aborted sequels to Jaws inspired movies like *Orca Part II*. As a bonus, all the Jaws rip-offs like *Grizzly* (1976) and *Tentacles* (1977) are reviewed. Hardcover (316 pp/5.83" X 8.27")/Softcover (340 pp/5.5" X 8.5") Suggested Retail: $29.99 (hc)/$17.95(sc) ISBN: 978-1-7344730-1-8

Classic Monsters Unmade covers lost and unmade films starring Dracula, Frankenstein, the Mummy and more monsters. Reviews unmade scripts like *The Return of Frankenstein* (1934) and *Wolf Man vs. Dracula* (1944). It also examines lost films of the silent era such as *The Werewolf* (1913) and *Drakula's Death* (1923). Softcover/Hardcover(428pp/5.83"X8.27") Suggested Retail: $22.99(sc)/ $27.99(hc)ISBN:978-1- 953221-85-8(hc)

Volume 2 explores the Hammer era and beyond, from unmade versions of *Brides of Dracula* (called *Disciple of Dracula*) to remakes of *Creature from the Black Lagoon*. Completely unmade films like *Kali: Devil Bride of Dracula* (1975) and *Godzilla vs. Frankenstein* (1964) are covered along with lost completed films like *Batman Fights Dracula* (1967) and *Black the Ripper* (1974). Coming Fall 2021.

NOSTALGIA

Written in the same spirit as *The Big Book of Japanese Giant Monster Movies*, this tome reviews all the classic Universal and Hammer horrors to star Dracula, Frankenstein, the Gillman and the rest along with obscure flicks like *The New Invisible Man* (1958), *Billy the Kid versus Dracula* (1966), *Blackenstein* (1973) and *Legend of the Werewolf* (1974). Coming 2021.

Written at an intermediate reading level for the kid in all of us, these picture books will take you back to your youth. In the spirit of the old Ian Thorne books are covered *Nabonga* (1944), *White Pongo* (1945) and more! Hardcover/Softcover (44 pp/7.5" X 9.25") Suggested Retail: $17.95(hc)/$9.99(sc) ISBN: 978- 1-7341546-9-6 (hc) 978- 1-7344730-5-6 (sc)

Written at an intermediate reading level for the kid in all of us, these picture books will take you back to your youth. In the spirit of the old Ian Thorne books are covered *The Lost World* (1925), *The Land That Time Forgot* (1975) and more! Hardcover/Softcover (44 pp/7.5" X 9.25") Suggested Retail: $17.95 (hc)/$9.99(sc) ISBN: 978-1-7344730 -6-3 (hc) 978-1-7344730-7-0 (sc)

Written at an intermediate reading level for the kid in all of us, these picture books will take you back to your youth. In the spirit of the old Ian Thorne books are covered *Them!* (1954), *Empire of the Ants* (1977) and more! Hardcover/Softcover (44 pp/7.5" X 9.25") $9.99(sc) ISBN: 978-1-7347816 -3-2 (hc) 978 -1-7347816-2-5 (sc)

THE BICEP BOOKS CATALOGUE

CRYPTOZOOLOGY/COWBOYS & SAURIANS

Cowboys & Saurians: Prehistoric Beasts as Seen by the Pioneers explores dinosaur sightings from the pioneer period via real newspaper reports from the time. Well-known cases like the Tombstone Thunderbird are covered along with more obscure cases like the Crosswicks Monster and more. Softcover (357 pp/5.06" X 7.8") Suggested Retail: $19.95 ISBN: 978-1-7341546-1-0

Cowboys & Saurians: Ice Age zeroes in on snowbound saurians like the Cerato-saurus of the Arctic Circle and a Tyrannosaurus of the Tundra, as well as sightings of Ice Age megafauna like mammoths, glyptodonts, Sarkastodons and Saber-toothed tigers. Tales of a land that time forgot in the Arctic are also covered. Softcover (264 pp/5.06" X 7.8") Suggested Retail: $14.99 ISBN: 978-1-7341546-7-2

Southerners & Saurians takes the series formula of exploring newspaper accounts of monsters in the pioneer period with an eye to the Old South. In addition to dinosaurs are covered Lizardmen, Frogmen, giant leeches and mosquitoes, and the Dingocroc, which might be an alien rather than a prehistoric survivor. Softcover (202 pp/5.06" X 7.8") Suggested Retail: $13.99 ISBN: 978-1-7344730-4-9

Cowboys & Saurians: South of the Border explores the saurians of Central and South America, like the Patagonian Plesiosaurus that was really a Iemisch, plus tales of the Neo-Mylodon (a giant ground sloth), a menacing monster from underground called the Minhocao, Glyptodonts, shark-men and even a three-headed dinosaur! Coming Summer 2021 ISBN: 978-1-953221-73-5

UFOLOGY/THE REAL COWBOYS & ALIENS IN CONJUNCTION WITH ROSWELL BOOKS

The Real Cowboys and Aliens: Early American UFOs explores UFO sightings in the USA between the years 1800-1864. Stories of encounters sometimes involved famous figures in U.S. history such as Lewis and Clark, and Thomas Jefferson.Hardcover (242pp/6" X 9") Softcover (262 pp/5.06" X 7.8") Suggested Retail: $24.99 (hc)/$15.95(sc) ISBN: 978-1-7341546-8-9\(hc)/978-1-7344730-8-7(sc)

The second entry in the series, Old West UFOs, covers reports spanning the years 1865-1895. Includes tales of Men in Black, Reptilians, Spring-Heeled Jack, Sasquatch from space, and other alien beings, in addition to the UFOs and airships. Hardcover (276 pp/6" X 9") Softcover (308 pp/5.06" X 7.8") Suggested Retail: $29.95 (hc)/$17.95(sc) ISBN: 978-1-7344730-0-1 (hc)/ 978-1-73447 30-2-5 (sc)

The third entry in the series, The Coming of the Airships, encompasses a short time frame with an incredibly high concentration of airship sightings between 1896-1899. The famous Aurora, Texas, UFO crash of 1897 is covered in depth along with many others. Hardcover (196 pp/6" X 9") Softcover (222 pp/5.06" X 7.8") Suggested Retail: $24.99 (hc)/$15.95(sc) ISBN: 978-1-7347816 -1-8 (hc)/978-1-7347816-0-1(sc)

Early 20th Century UFOs kicks off a new series that investigates UFO sightings of the early 1900s. Includes tales of UFOs sighted over the Titanic as it sank, Nikola Tesla receiving messages from the stars, an alien being found encased in ice, and a possible virus from outer space!Hardcover (196 pp/6" X 9") Softcover (222 pp/5.06" X 7.8") Suggested Retail: $27.99 (hc)/$16.95(sc) ISBN: 978-1-7347816-1-8 (hc)/978-1-73478 16-0-1(sc)

BACK ISSUES

THE LOST FILMS FANZINE

ISSUE #1 SPRING 2020 The lost Italian cut of *Legend of Dinosaurs and Monster Birds* called *Terremoto 10 Grado*, plus *Bride of Dr. Phibes* script, *Good Luck! Godzilla*, the King Kong remake that became a car commercial, Bollywood's lost *Jaws* rip-off, Top Ten Best Fan Made Godzilla trailers plus an interview with Scott David Lister. 60 pages. Three variant covers/editions (premium color/basic color/b&w)

ISSUE #2 SUMMER 2020 How 1935's *The Capture of Tarzan* became 1936's *Tarzan Escapes*, the Orca sequels that weren't, Baragon in Bollywood's *One Million B.C.*, unmade *Kolchak: The Night Stalker* movies, *The Norliss Tapes*, *Superman V: The New Movie*, why there were no *Curse of the Pink Panther* sequels, *Moonlight Mask: The Movie*. 64 pages. Two covers/editions (basic color/b&w)

ISSUE #3 FALL 2020 Blob sequels both forgotten and unproduced, *Horror of Dracula* uncut, *Frankenstein Meets the Wolfman* and talks, myths of the lost *King Kong* Spider-Pit sequence debunked, the *Carnosaur* novel vs. the movies, *Terror in the Streets* 50th anniversary, *Bride of Godzilla* 55th Unniversary, Lee Powers sketchbook. 100 pages. Two covers/editions (basic color/b&w)

ISSUE #4 WINTER 2020/21 *Diamonds Are Forever's* first draft with Goldfinger, *Disciple of Dracula* into *Brides of Dracula*, *War of the Worlds That Weren't* Part II, *Day the Earth Stood Still II* by Ray Bradbury, *Deathwish 6*, *Atomic War Bride*, *What Am I Doing in the Middle of a Revolution?*, *Spring Dream in the Old Capital* and more. 70 pages. Two covers/editions (basic color/b&w)

MOVIE MILESTONES

ISSUE #1 AUGUST 2020 Debut issue celebrating 80 years of *One Million B.C.* (1940), and an early 55th Anniversary for *One Million Years B.C.* (1966). Abandoned ideas, casting changes, and deleted scenes are covered, plus, a mini-B.C. stock-footage filmography and much more! 54 pages. Three collectible covers/editions (premium color/basic color/b&w)

ISSUE #2 OCTOBER 2020 Celebrates the joint 50th Anniversaries of *When Dinosaurs Ruled the Earth* (1970) and *Creatures the World Forgot* (1971). Also includes looks at *Prehistoric Women* (1967), *When Women Had Tails* (1970), and *Caveman* (1981), plus unmade films like *When the World Cracked Open.* 72 pages. Three collectible covers/editions (premium color/basic color/b&w)

ISSUE #3 WINTER 2021 Japanese 'Panic Movies' like *The Last War* (1961), *Submersion of Japan* (1973), and *Bullet Train* (1975) are covered on celebrated author Sakyo Komatsu's 90th birthday. The famous banned Toho film *Prophecies of Nostradamus* (1974) are also covered. 124 pages. Three collectible editions (premium color/ basic color/ b&w)

ISSUE #4 SPRING 2021 This issue celebrates the joint 60th Anniversaries of *Gorgo*, *Reptilicus* and *Konga* examining unmade sequels like *Reptilicus 2*, and other related lost projects like *Kuru Island* and *The Volcano Monsters.* Also explores the Gorgo, Konga and Reptilicus comic books from Charlton. 72 pages. Three collectible covers/editions (premium color/basic color/b&w)

NEXT ISSUE!!!

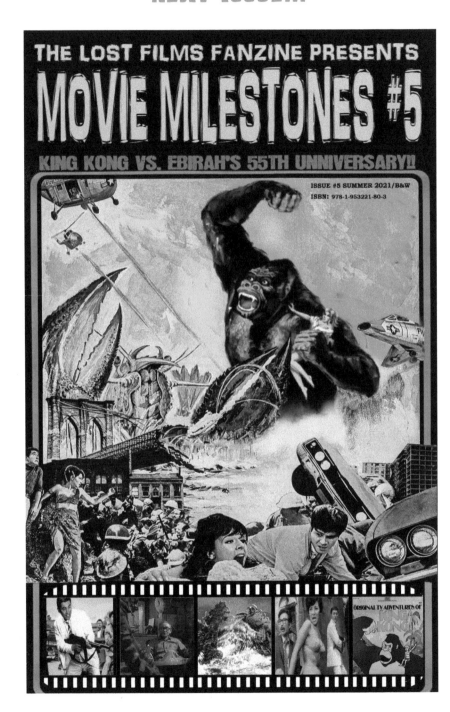

THE LOST FILMS FANZINE PRESENTS

MOVIE MILESTONES #5

KING KONG VS. EBIRAH'S 55TH UNNIVERSARY!!

ISSUE #5 SUMMER 2021/B&W
ISBN: 978-1-953221-80-3

ORIGINAL TV ADVENTURES OF